Standing Watch
The Fire Towers of Arizona

Eileen Moore

Published by
Morten Moore Publishing

Non Liability Statement

When we began to research this book, I made the decision to exclude information on the exact location of each tower. This was done in part to protect the lookouts and in part to allow them the privacy to do their jobs without greatly increasing the number of visitors to their towers. We understand that visitors will still make their way along dusty back roads and up narrow one lane roads to oogle these aging structures and momentarily distract the lookouts.

If you should choose to visit some of these fire towers, it is your responsibility to check with the Forest Service or governing agency on access and to travel to and from these structures responsibly. It is the responsibility of each visitor to use good judgement and make wise decisions regarding their activities. The author and all associated with this book, directly or indirectly, disclaim any liability for accidents, injuries, damages or losses which may occur when using this book. The responsibility for safety remains with the individual.

If you choose to visit some of these towers, we recommend that you check with the lookout before climbing the stairway. They may be unable or unwilling to have visitors during your visit to the site. Please politely follow any instructions that they may give in regard to your safety.

We wish you the very best experience while enjoying God's creation and the works of man scattered throughout our beautiful forests!

Published by Morten Moore Publishing
P.O. Box 881
Flagstaff, Az 86002

©Ruth Eileen & Ken Mortenson
All rights reserved
First Edition 2006
ISBN 0-9672576-1-1

Library of Congress
2007902792

Table of Contents

Introduction
A Very Brief History of the Forest Service and Fire Prevention.
Fire Tower Styles and Construction
page 3

Chapter 1
The Towers of the National Park Service
Special Feature: The Civilian Conservation Corp
page 19

Chapter 2
The Towers of the Bureau of Land Management
page 37

Chapter 3
The Tower for the Hualapai Reservation
page 43

Chapter 4
The Towers of the North and South Kaibab National Forest
Special Feature: The Tree Towers of the North Kaibab
and the Grand Canyon National Park
page 47

Chapter 5
The Towers of the Coconino National Forest
Special Feature: The Radio Fire
page 73

Chapter 6
The Towers of the Navajo Nation
Special Feature: Native Forestry
page 103

Chapter 7
The Towers of the Apache - Sitgreaves National Forest
Special Feature: The Rodeo-Chediski Fire & the Fire Towers
page 119

Chapter 8
The Towers of the White Mountain Apache / Fort Apache Reservation
Special Feature: The Road to Limestone
page 157

Chapter 9
The Towers of the San Carlos Apache Reservation
Special Feature: The Geronimo Hot Shots
page 173

Chapter 10
The Towers of the Tonto National Forest
page 185

Chapter 11
The Towers of the Prescott National Forest
page 201

Chapter 12
The Towers of the Coronado National Forest
Special Features: Working Together in Very Close Quarters
Ladybugs!
page 215

Chapter 13
The View from the Outhouse.
page 241

Index
page 248

Acknowledgements

In the five decades that I have traveled this earth, I thank those who have stood watch over me with their concern, their prayers and their encouragement. To each of you, from my heart - thank you!

My thanks to my husband for his love and support as we traveled dusty roads and hiked steep hills. Thank you for how you have grown in your love for me and for your support of our adventures.

Thank you to each of the lookouts and forestry personnel who patiently answered my questions and tolerated my presence. Thank you for your insights and your willingness to share this part of your lives.

And, to my father, Don Caswell. Thank you for insisting that I learn to write clearly and precisely. Thank you for your help with editing the copy and your encouragement to me in the midst of your own battle.

I owe a special thanks to David Lorentz. Dave is regarded as the foremost authority on fire towers in the state of Arizona. He has spent years researching the archives of the National Forests and Special Collections found throughout the state. He has visited all of the towers of Arizona and New Mexico, most of them multiple times. He has spent hours talking with those who stand watch as well as fire management officials and other personnel. He continues to update this information each year. He actively pursues dismantled tower sites that have been forgotten, the foundations slowly eroding in Arizona's climate.

And he fields phone calls from curious reporters and writers as well as those who wish to visit the towers. I waited till I had visited every tower and had completed much of my research before talking to Dave. He generously updated my research on tower statistics and shared his own experiences. His research, which I found before even meeting the man, made this book much easier to write.

He has left a trail for those who follow. We have much to live up to in his meticulous scholarship. Thank you, Dave!

Fire Towers

Apache Sitgreaves NF
1. Bear Mountain
2. Big Lake
3. Blue
4. Deer Springs
5. Escudilla
6. Gentry
7. Greens Peak
8. Juniper Ridge
9. Lake Mountain
10. O'Haco
11. PS Knoll
12. Promontory
13. Reno
14. Rose Peak
15. Springer Mountain

Coconino
16. Apache Maid
17. Baker Butte
18. Buck Mountain
19. East Pocket
20. Eldon
21. Hutch Mountain
22. Lee Butte
23. Moqui
24. Mormon Mountain
25. O'Leary
26. Turkey Butte
27. Woody Mountain

Coronado
28. Atascosa
29. Barfoot
30. Heliograph
31. Lemmon Rock
32. Mt. Bigelow
33. Monte Vista
34. Red Mountain
35. Webb Peak
36. WestPeak

Kaibab
37. Big Springs
38. Bill Williams
39. Dry Park
40. Grand View
41. Jacob Lake
42. Kendrick
43. Red Butte
44. Red Hill
45. Round Mountain
46. Volunteer

Prescott
47. Horse Thief
48. Hyde Mountain
49. Mingus
50. Mount Union
51. Spruce Mountain
52. Towers

Tonto
53. Aztec
54. Colcord
55. Diamond Point
56. Humboldt
57. McFadden Peak
58. Mount Ord
59. Signal Peak

Bureau of Land Management
60. Black Rock
61. Whitney Pass

National Parks & Monuments
62. Happy Valley
63. Hopi
64. Kanabownitz
65. North Rim
66. Signal Hill
67. Sugar Loaf

Navajo Reservation
68. Black Pinnackle
69. Fluted Rock
70. Oak Ridge
71. Piney Hill
72. Roof Butte

Fort Apache & San Carlos
73. Buckskin
74. Chediski
75. Limestone
76. Maverick
77. McKay Peak
78. Odart

San Carlos
79. Dry Lake
80. Hilltop

Hualapai
81. Thornton

Arizona Map

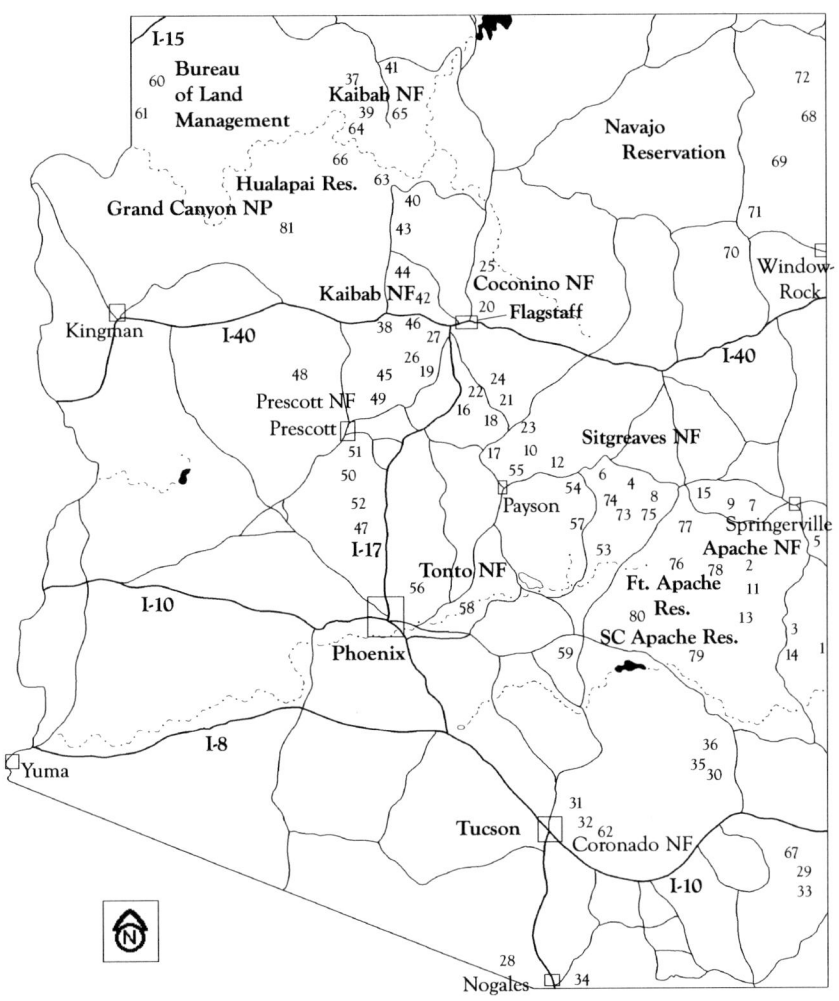

Arizona's
Fire Towers & Cabins

In Honor of
Marty Mortenson
1983 - 2005

Beloved Son, much missed, never forgotten.

Isaiah 57:1 & 2
The righeous perish, and no one ponders it in his heart;
devout men are taken away and no one understands
that the righteous are taken away to be spared from evil.
Those who walk uprightly enter into peace;
they find rest as they lie in death.

To a son, who as he grew, took on the role of looking out for his mom in the wild places of Arizona. A brother, who stood for up his sisters and admired his dad. A Marine, who looked out for the Marine on his left and on his right, mentoring one who came behind. He understood what it meant to stand watch on those who were weaker and less able.

Other books by Eileen Moore

Arizona Trails for Children

Foreword

Why write a book about fire towers? My interest in fire towers began while hiking throughout Arizona. As we hiked up a peak we would stumble across a tower, sometimes occupied. As we visited with the men and women who work in the towers my admiration only grew as I heard how seriously they took their jobs. It wasn't hard to recognize the importance of what they did in helping to preserve the wilderness areas for all to enjoy. They stand watch on our behalf.

Many people are not aware the towers exist. When I asked one woman if she had seen a 'lookout' near where we stood, she insisted that I had to see the view from a pile of rocks just below the peak. She had never heard of the fire towers and was completely unaware of the existence of one within a quarter mile. Even when we become aware of a tower, few of us stop to say thank you to the lookout for his efforts, often performed under less than ideal conditions.

These structures also have a historical interest: many of the towers date back to the 1930s, an era of desperation for many people who struggled to keep body and soul together. The Aermotor towers are take us back to the era of the Civilian Conservation Corp and encourage us to think about how far we have come in conservation and forest management.

I thought a book might help to bring public attention to the towers and give people a greater appreciation of their role today. The book serves as a tribute to these silent monuments of another era and to the men and women who serve the greater society in standing watch.

You may note that the book does not include directions to the towers. There are two reasons for this. The lookouts have a job to do. Primarily they are looking for plumes of smoke rising above the trees, ready to call the dispatch center to report a fire. While their secondary role is to help educate the public about the wilderness, they do not need to be distracted from their watch. One lookout grumbled that such a book would further increase the large number of visitors that already inundate her tower near the Grand Canyon. There are times when she closes the door to allow herself time to recover from the endless stream of repetitive questions. " How tall is the tower? So what are you doing up here? Are there any

1

fires out there?"

But there is a second reason to be concerned about publicizing the location of the towers. Not all of the visitors have good intentions in visiting these remote locations. They may simply vandalize a site, others may intend harm to the lookouts. The lack of public knowledge about the location of the towers may give the lookouts some security, particularly the women, allowing them to safely do their jobs. I have come across some strange stories on some of our towers: lookouts have had visitors in the middle of the night, coming over the railings of their catwalks. The lookouts cannot understand why someone dressed in black would need to visit the lookout in the middle of the night, shunning the stairway or calling for help from the ground. Consequently, we chose not to list the exact locations of the towers and cabins.

If you want to visit a tower, I hope it is an enjoyable and educational experience. Call your local Forest Service office and they may direct you to a tower. Or you can pick up a forest service map, locating for yourself the towers and access roads. Be sure to ask about road conditions before venturing out. Be aware that many of the roads have locked gates about half mile below the tower that require visitors to hike to the site. Above all else, in visiting a tower, be respectful of the men and women who serve in these lonely posts. Do as they ask for they have the authority to call in law enforcement officials. Their authority extends over the tower and the terrain. When you leave, take a moment to say thank you as they are standing watch for you.

Introduction

Driving along a dirt road toward a fire tower, I never quite know what to expect. Will I find a spartan forty five foot Aermotor with a tiny cab or a forest giant, firmly planted in the rock, topped by a live-in twelve by twelve foot cab with modern appliances? Or maybe a throwback, not even a tower but a simple cabin on a rocky knob like Lemmon Rock. It is a bit of a mystery.

Walk through the wood frame door and the view seizes you, its scope magnificently spread at your feet. Each tower seemed to hold something new, either in the structure or the region it covers. Often, the people on watch in the towers are interesting with a variety of life experiences behind them. I have come to respect the lookouts, each so distinct but with a common goal of giving something back to the society from which they first grew. Some of them came with no experience. Some so unprepared in their first year that they didn't own a car, in which to drive the long access to their duty station. Others have watched the years pass and trained other lookouts to stand watch.

It was the actual towers that first drew me. Lonely sentinels in wind-swept outposts, unrecognized by those they protect, clustered in the valleys below. As I visited the towers, I began to see the differences in construction and I could guess the era in which they had been built in a single glance. I gained an appreciation for the history represented in the different eras of the fire towers. And I thought their contribution should be recognized as the structures age another year, coming closer to the time when they will be replaced by technology or at least a new structure.

Fire has been recognized for its power to transform the landscape around us. Over the centuries, since fire was first used to cook raw meat, to warm a cold body, we have struggled to maintain control over a thing that can create such destruction across beautiful landscapes. Yet, when under control, fire can still be used to make our lives more comfortable.

As the settlers first moved away from the eastern seaboard, they encountered the heavy forests that swept from the northern climes above the great lakes, along the Appalachian Mountains into the southeast. They saw the heavy timber as a barrier to westward expansion and to their desires to cultivate the soil. Fire was both the enemy and a tool for clearing the forests. Across the great plains, the grassland fires were terrible for the settlers living in sod houses, distant from neighbors and the small communities where people might band together to form fire lines against the raging flames.

As the caravans of white-topped Conestoga wagons moved across the plains, it seemed the land was boundless. It would take centuries before the plains were brought to the level of domesticity represented by the first colonies founded in this new land. To encourage development in the west, Congress enacted the Homestead Act in 1862. This allowed an adult, male or female, to stake claim on 160 acres for five years. In that time they were to make specified improvements which included building a home, cultivating a minimum amount of acreage and planting trees. They had to provide a source of water for their homestead and live on it for the majority of five years. When this was completed they could claim the title to the land under their own names. Thousands of people poured from the crowded, dirty cities of the eastern United States, many of them with little knowledge of how to actually accomplish these improvements or to cultivate the soil. It was an opportunity to improve their station in life by hard work. There were no guarantees and this often proved a disaster for both the homesteader and the land he claimed.

In the late 1800s, a national conservation movement began to flourish and concern for preserving the remaining wilderness began to effect national policy. In 1891, Congress passed the General Land Revision Act. The Act granted the President the authority to publically designate and set aside specified areas of forested public lands as Forest Reserves. Unfortunately, this did not always take into account the claims of many of the early settlers or those who claimed land under the Homestead Act. Settlers who thought they had clear title to the land, found the federally declared Forest Reserves might usurp their rights to what they had worked so hard to claim. In the years that followed thirteen Reserves were created in Arizona.

1893	Grand Canyon Forest Reserve
1989	Black Mesa Forest Reserve
	Prescott Forest Reserve
	San Francisco Mountain Forest Reserve
1902	Santa Rita Forest Reserve

	Santa Catalina Forest Reserve
	Chiricahua Forest Reserve
1905	Tonto Forest Reserve
1906	Baboquivari Forest Reserve
	Huachuca Forest Reserve
	Tumacacori Forest Reserve
	Peloncillo Forest Reserve
1907	Verde Forest Reserve

The federal government employed rangers to ride patrols throughout the forest reserves and regulate any activity, including the timber industry, ranching and recreation. Many of the early lookout sites were first established by the Reserve rangers. They found high points within their region and frequently rode or climbed to a higher elevation in scouting for plumes of smoke rising above the forest.

In 1905, the United States Forest Service was created to preserve and protect what had previously been the Forest Reserves. This clearly placed the responsibility for our public lands with the federal government rather than under state authority though in the west the states still retained significant acreage under their control. After 1905, the Conservation movement continued, though sometimes along a different path than the Forest Service. In the late 1900's the two were publically at odds over a number of issues and how to best preserve the remaining wilderness.

In the early years of the Forest Service, Arthur Ringland, the first District Forester in the Southwest Region, supervised the systematic expansion of the network of fire towers and cabins for the purpose of preventing fires. Some of these were built at the same sites that had been used by the early rangers within the Forest Reserves. The rangers had ridden through their districts, stopping at high points, to observe the landscape and check for columns of smoke rising above the forest canopy. At some sites, an alilade was mounted on a post to improve observation. Once the location of a column of smoke was determined, a patrol member would ride to the smoke and put out the fire. Unfortunately, once the patrol dropped below the forest canopy, finding the fire was not always easy. He might require an additional sighting and climb a tall tree to look for the smoke above the tree tops. If it proved to be beyond his capacity to control, he hired local people to help fight the fire. Frequently, ranchers and logging crews would respond on their own after a fire broke out near their camps.

In 1910 devastating fires swept through the forests of the northwest and Congress quickly authorized more funding to fight forest fires. In 1911, Congress passed the Weeks Act that provided more funding for fire control and state cooperative fire prevention programs as well as more research. This was followed by the Clarke-McNary Act which expanded federal assistance to the states for fire control programs. The Forest Service increased the number of fire towers, supervisors hired seasonal crews of men to fight the wild fires rather than relying on local residents. The funds from the Clarke-McNary Act helped pay the seasonal wages of fire look outs over the next 50 years.

Ranger using alilade from high point above forest.
Photos: GCNP archives.

The earliest towers were crow's nests, a wooden platform either standing alone or at the top of tall trees. The design included a central vertical beam with cross braces extending outward, set at 45 degrees to a platform mounted on a central pole or tree. In time, the Forest Service began to build towers with four corner posts that were cut from the forests and sunk upright into pits. In the old wood towers, eight inch square beams were frequently used for the main posts while three by six inch cross beams were used for the diagonal supports. A platform was constructed across the top of the posts for observation. Usually a handrail was constructed around the platform and an alilade mounted on the platform to improve locating

the position of the fire. The lookouts sat on the platform, exposed to the elements, hot sun or drizzling rain, until the Forest Service began to enclose some of these platforms.

The L4 model with a fourteen-foot square cabin became popular in the 1920s. The cabin sat at ground level on a prominent point overlooking a panoramic view. The L-5 was a ten-foot square version of the L-4. A number of these survive in Arizona but most are used on an emergency basis only. The D-6 was a fourteen-foot square cabin with a cupola built above the living space for observation. Only a few were built in Arizona and none of these exist in Arizona today.

As the country sank into the Great Depression of the 1920's with nearly twenty-five percent of our population unemployed, President Franklin Roosevelt proposed sending our young men into the rural areas to make

Crows Nest with observer.

Photo: GCNP Archives

improvements on our roads, parks and recreational areas. The plan served not only to improve our public lands but also put a large number of unemployed young men to work. The Emergency Work Program spawned the Civilian Conservation Corp and became an instrument of change throughout the country. The Forest Service, with the CCC work force, could implement the changes that had been brewing through the conservation movement of the 1800s. When it came to fire prevention, the Forest Service had the personnel to build fire towers and other structures along with campgrounds and access roads throughout our national forests. The CCC also built cabins, storage sheds, outhouses and corrals near many of the towers for the comfort of lookouts stationed in remote locations. The majority of our fire towers were built in this era and many still stand today, listed on the National Historic Register. Others have been dismantled or replaced with more modern structures.

In the 1930's, the towers were no longer designed and constructed at the local level. Instead, companies that had once manufactured windmills for the farming and ranching communities, now turned to fire towers. The Forest Service found the steel towers were less expensive to erect and to maintain. The Aermotor Company cut the material for thousands of fire towers across the country. The Pacific Steel Company and the International Derrick Company also supplied material for these towers within Arizona. The materials were delivered to a railhead, such as Flagstaff in northern Arizona, and then shipped by wagon to the site where they were constructed by the CCC or Forest Service crews.

Building Hopi Fire Tower.   Photo: GCNP Archives

Approaching an old Aermotor tower, the design is unmistakable. Narrow steel angle rises at the four corners with cross beams stretched between the four corner supports. Between the cross beams, additional angle steel is set diagonally in either an 'X', 'Z' or a 'K' pattern. At first, a ladder was built up the outside of the frame to the cab at the top. Later, Aermotor began to construct a stairway up the center of the tower to the cab, with the size of the platforms shrinking between each flight as they gained in elevation. The steps were either wood, expanded metal or preforated metal plates. At the top, the metal cab was a standard seven by seven-foot square, the entrance through a trapdoor in the wood floor. This did not leave much room for the lookout to move around throughout the day.

The Forest Service would later adopt a similar design but increase the size of the cab to ten by ten or twelve by twelve feet, allowing the lookout to live in the cab. Catwalks around the outside of the cab were also

Osbourne
Fire
Finder

added on later models, allowing the lookout to enter the cab through a standard door on the side rather than a trapdoor in the floor. Forest Service models included the R-6 flat usually mounted on the CL100-106 tower.

At the center of the cab was placed the Osbourne Fire Finder. This instrument was developed by William Osbourne in 1911 and proved to be a great improvement over the simple alilade. The instrument was a round table, divided into 360 degrees around the circumference, set on a cast iron base.. Mounted on either side of the circle and allowed to rotate around a map affixed to the plate were two instruments. One was a narrow metal piece with a slot down the center, the second a metal piece with a cross hair mounted in a wider metal slot. The lookout would align the two metal pieces in the direction of a column of smoke and sight through the narrow slot at the cross hairs. Once the slot lined up with the cross hairs in the direction of the smoke, he would take a reading based on the 360 degrees marked around the edge of the circular table. The reading corresponded to a circle drawn on a Forest Service map with the tower at the center of the circle on a north-south axis. The reading matched a duplicate map at headquarters and using the information, the dispatch center would send crews to the proper location of the fire. It was a little tricker to report the distance from the tower. The instruments might help to indicate distance but lookouts often refined their reports regarding distance as their experience grew with each year. Some lookouts take it as a challenge to get the distance right when ridges block the horizon, leaving only a column of smoke against the horizon without corresponding landmarks.

The key to accurately locating the fires lay in the triangulation of corresponding reports between towers. With each tower calling in the location based on readings from his site, the district could quickly lay down a series of lines from each tower that crossed at the site of the blaze.

Recently, the Coronado National Forest had to replace one of its fire finders and found that only one company still manufactures the unit.

The history of fire towers in this country falls into three distinct categories. There is the period that stretches from 1905 to 1929 with the Forest Service designing and constructing many of their facilities under local district guidelines. This left a wide range of design specifications in the structures that date to this period. The old style of cabin with a cupola mounted on the roof dates to this era.

The second period belongs to the 1930s, ending in 1942, when the Civilian Conservation Corp was disbanded and the country entered World War II. These structures erected during this era were narrow, limited towers that utilized a minimal amount of steel and featured tiny cabs. The towers were built to uniform specifications based on old windmill design. The third period stretches from 1945 into the 1980s with the Forest Service constructing the towers and cabin based on standard federal design criterion. Structures of this era are much more solid, larger in design and often include modern conveniences like kitchen counters, appliances and bunk beds. These larger towers often replaced older models built during the previous forty years. The largest cabs were usually mounted on a cement block base and only rose one story above ground level. Compared to the tiny Aermotor cabs, these cinder block-based buildings seemed spacious. After the 1980's, almost no structures have been built for the exclusive purpose of forest observation.

To understand the challenge of wildfire for forest managers in Arizona, we must look at our climate and terrain. Arizona has six broadly based life zones defined by the predominant vegetation in each zone. The lowest in elevation at around 1,500 feet is desert scrub, characterized by the cactus and sage brush, with isolated paloverde trees. Rising in elevations, grasslands make an appearance through frequently the line between desert scrub and grassland can be a bit indistinct. The grasslands meld into a woodland of pinon and juniper life zone around 5,000 feet elevation. Some scientists would place a separate chaparral between the grasslands and the pinon-juniper. At 5,000 feet, the trees are frequently wide spread due to a limited amount of rainfall and poor soil.

The ponderosa pine zone is present at about the 7,000 foot elevation, followed by the fir and spruce at 8,000 to 11,000 feet above sea level. The final zone is above the tree line where the tundra replaces the trees, reaching to the bare rock generally above 12,000 feet.

The amount of rainfall each zone receives varies widely but generally the life zones above 5,000 feet receive more rainfall than the desert and in turn 7,000 to 10,000 feet elevation receives more than the pinon juniper life zone. In Arizona we have two fairly predictable periods of rain or snowfall. The winter months can see heavy snowfall in the highlands though more recently, measurable precipitation has been a bit scanty. In the summer, the winds shift and moisture flows up from the Gulf of Mexico bringing summer rains to much of Arizona for about two months. In the 1980s, Arizona was blessed with abundant precipitation in both seasons. But with the mid-1990s, rain and snow fall have decreased, leaving us in drought.

Despite the cyclical periods of moisture entering the state, Arizona has earns its name as an arid zone. Even the highlands can be dry when compared to the wet climates of the northwest. When the summer rains move in with intense displays of lightening striking into the tinder dry forests, wildfires break out across the terrain. In years of drought, the conditions are prime for the flames to sweep through forests devastated by a lack of moisture and now the bark beetle.

Whether fire has been seen as a destructive force of nature or a tool to thin the undergrowth, fire towers have played an important role. In the early days, lookouts reported the smoke sightings with the intention of fire prevention. In more recent years, the fires would be allowed to burn with the goal of thinning the underbrush and small trees below the forest canopy. Forest managers monitored the fires to ensure that they did not roar out of control, turning the terrain into a moonscape. The lookouts often served an important role in monitoring the smoke, reporting changes that indicated whether the fire might make a run into something more dangerous.

In the 1980's a new way of thinking about the role of fire began to surface. The Forest Service had struggled to prevent fire from destroying vast timber reserves by suppressing all fires. As a result, forests throughout the country had become overgrown. When fires did make their run, the effort to suppress them required ever great effort and resources. Instead of creeping through the underbrush, the flames now swept through the forest canopy. The fires burned with more intensity, sometimes leaving the terrain a moonscape. This is not to say that such devastation did not occur before man began to actively manage the forest. Early records describe the scars of a fire in the San Francisco Mountains that burned over 18,000 acres long before white men settled in the southwest. But now the fires were becoming more frequent and more catastrophic.

Researchers began to theorize that fire should be used therapeutically to clear out the underbrush. Thickets of small pines, each struggling for available sunlight would be cut and removed. These theories were put into practice in northern Arizona by researchers at Northern Arizona University. The results were good. Grass for the wildlife flourished in the wake of a controlled burn, the threat of catastrophic fire was reduced, the forest regained its multi-level canopy. Some wildlife managers did question whether too many dog-hair thickets of pines were being removed and how this effected the wildlife. But overall the pattern began to spread to other forests as forest managers practiced what had proven successful in Arizona. This change in policy also effected the towers. Some were removed permanently while the role of the lookouts was somewhat altered.

When visitors approach a tower, one of their first questions seems to always be, "how tall is this tower?" The standard formula measures the tower from the base of the stairs to the floor of the cab for the height of the tower. The base and the height of the cab are not considered part of the manufacturer's given height. When visiting a fire tower, if one is unsure of the height, it is fairly simple to count the number of steps and multiply that number times the height of the risers between each step. For example the risers may be eight inches in height and there may be a total of sixty stairs. Multiply 60 times 8 inches and then divide by 12 and we have the height of forty feet. This may be a bit more complicated if the risers are of varying heights or if a ladder is part of the staircase.

While these structures have stood the test of climate and even wildfire, it is the people who are the variables in the equation. It is the people who bring life to the cold steel and gritty wood structures. It is the human spirit within the tower to whom the responsibility is given to stand watch over creation. It is a responsibility that stretches back to the very beginning of the world when the creator designated man as the high point of creation, to care for our planet. How fitting that it is man, in the image of the creator, who sits above the treetops, overlooking ridges and valleys, ready to spring into action at the first sign of change to alter the course of history.

The primary job of the lookout is to stand watch over the forests. With time, as outdoor activity has increased, the role of the lookout as interpreter has also become important in interacting with the public. It is important however to remember in visiting a fire tower that the lookout's first responsibility is to the forest and as such he may choose not to interact with visitors.

Most lookouts stand watch five to six days a week with a relief lookout coming to the site to relieve them for their time off. During the most active part of the season, before the seasonal rains arrive to dampen the forest, the lookout may stand watch as long as thirteen hours in a twenty-four hours period. That means the lookout may arrive in the cab at 8:00 in the morning and not go off duty until 9:00 at night if the conditions require him to remain longer than an eight hour shift. The lookout is responsible for his tower and has the authority to bar the public from the structure and any outlying structures as well.

While some lookouts see the job as a position to earn an income during the summer months, for others it is their prime source of income throughout the year. All would agree that whatever the level of income, they are there to serve the public good. They are giving back a little to a society that has given them much. In a society that is driven by the need to consider oneself of primary importance to all other considerations, here is a group of people that have arrived at the understanding that they can benefit the greater good by offering themselves to stand watch over the rest of us. In that role, they protect us from wildfire or from ourselves when we get a little crazy with all that fresh air and unconfined living. Each one has a different story to tell, a different road to their time in the fire tower but they share the common goal of looking out for the rest of us. They confine themselves to tiny cabs, often in primitive conditions that most of us would hesitate to tolerate in our homes. They may or may not rejoice in the lack of human companionship. They may tolerate rude attitudes or even suffer vandalism at the hands of the criminally-minded individual. They often tell some great stories when given a little time in the company of one who is willing to listen.

They are a unique group of people who may prolong a time that is coming to an end in the face of technology. There is a quiet debate about whether fire towers and their lookouts have served a purpose that can now be replaced by more modern methods. Some argue that it is time to relegate the lookout and the fire tower to history. The reasons are varied. Some argue that more fire reports are coming in from the general public and that aerial reconnaissance has proven to be effective. Radio repeaters along with better roads and ground transportation have reduced the response time to the fires that are reported. Some argue that inflation in the costs of operation and maintaining the towers is prohibitive though one might wonder about the cost of aerial reconnaissance. Changes in policy about forest management have also been offered as a reason to cut back on the number of towers required in many regions. New wilderness designations do not include the foreign structures within their boundaries. And finally there is some concern about our litigious society and the increasing cost of liability in operating these aging structures.

The lookouts scoff at those who decry the need for towers and insist their job will always be required if the forest is to be maintained properly. To those who question the value of the towers in a modern society, I would argue that the towers are a fixed point of stable communication and assistance in the vast forest, a source of help when problems develop along dusty roads. Visitors can seek help from a lookout when they are miles from civilization. The observation and willing attitudes from the lookouts are of great value in a society where personal safety is threatened by the increasing alienation of the individual in the face of our advancing technology. Human discernment and compassion have yet to be replaced by a mircro chip.

Each year more towers are removed as the climate takes its toll. The remaining towers continue to provide shelter to their lookouts in season and out, year after year. The one complaint is that budgets have been stretched so thin that there is little money to perform maintenance on the towers. With the restrictions from the National Historic Register, many of the 1930 era towers need more than a coat of paint if they are to be safe and properly cared for against the ravages of time. Many lookouts make minor repairs without reporting the cost of supplies to their managers.

So what do these towers represent today. They are both a necessary tool in our forest management as well as a symbol of a slower paced era. They stand watch over a society that increasingly bears the scars of ever increasing violence and personal adulation. They stand watch while the rest of us go about our lives unaware that there is someone watching out on our behalf.

A note on the men and women who work the fire towers.

In most states, when referring to the fire towers, the terms fire tower and lookout are interchangable. In Arizona, the terms are generally not interchangable. Fire tower refers to the structure whereas the lookout is the person in the tower. We have tried to maintain that understanding in this manuscript.

Most lookouts are quietly content with their positions. They are often retired or use the position to fill in the summer months, working elsewhere during the winter.

The one complaint I frequently heard from lookouts was the deterioration of the towers with no money in tight budgets to do the necessary repairs. This is a common complaint in public agencies across the country.

Some lookouts may quietly question the decisions of superiors but would never voice their doubts to the public. Some feel they have not been treated fairly on the location and choice of towers. As the number of fire towers to be manned is reduced by tight budgets and changes in forest management, the competition for the better towers can be intense.

But overall, the lookouts may be one of the most content groups of public agency employees in the country. They are hospitable, open to lively conversations with a willingness to offer assistance in the face of formidable challenges. Many of them frequently display a wonderful sense of humor. It has been a pleasure to meet each one of them.

North Rim cabin, once home to lookout Edward Abby.

National Park Service

Chapter 1

In Arizona, the National Park Service maintains and manages twenty National Parks and Monuments. Three of these have a fire tower or cabin within their borders.

The Sahuaro National Monument is located on both the eastern and western borders of Tucson, sharing a common border with the Catalina district of the Coronado National Monument. The Monument is located in a desert ecological zone yet its boundaries extend into the Rincon Mountains, reaching an elevation of 8,482 feet at Rincon Peak. Happy Valley Fire Cabin is located in the Monument.

The Chiricahua National Monument is in the far southeastern corner of Arizona. The Wilderness of Rocks, a forest of rock hoodoos, is under the watch of the Sugar Loaf Peak fire cabin.

The Grand Canyon National Park slices through the northwestern section of the state, stretching 277 miles from Lees Ferry to the Grand Wash Cliffs. Much of the land under Park Service management, within the canyon, is barren of vegetation. On the north rim of the Grand Canyon and sections of the southern rim, heavily forested park land is only distinguished from National Forest land by a barb wire fence.

Four towers stand on the north and south rims of the Grand Canyon. Three of the four towers date from the 1930-1940 era of the Civilian Conservation Corp. None of them are currently used for observation as the Park Service has begun to rely on aerial observation, smoke reports from visitors in the back country and smoke sightings by Forest Service lookouts. They remain of historical interest for those who seek them out.

This is the case for many of the monuments in Arizona. Close proximity to Forest Service lands and visitor reports allow the Park Service to eliminate the use of fire towers on their lands.

Happy Valley / National Park Service

Happy Valley Cabin with a member of a fire crew.
Photos: Sahuaro National Monument

Tower: Happy Valley
Year Built: 1969
Height: 3'
Manufacture: USDA Forest Service
Model: L-4 house
Elevation: 7,348'
National Park: Sahuaro National Monument East
Access: Trail
Rating: Inactive

A 100 foot tower once stood at the summit of Mica Peak. It was removed in 1985 and moved piece by piece to Tucson though its current location is unknown.

Happy Valley

Happy Valley Fire Cabin looks out over the Rincon Mountains and the Sahuaro National Monument. The original cabin was built in 1904 by Levi Howell Manning as a summer retreat at Manning Camp. He served as Surveyor General of the Arizona Territory and later became the Mayor of Tucson. After the original cabin was removed, an L-4 cabin was built in 1969 by the Forest Service on Heartbreak Ridge between Rincon and Mica Peaks. When Sahuaro National Monument was established, the cabin came under the auspices of the National Park Service.

The fourteen foot square cabin on Heartbreak Ridge is no longer actively used as a fire cabin. When it was actively used, the Forest Service frequently assigned a married couple or a family to the site. Lookouts hiked six miles from the trail head to the site and the Park Service seemed to believe that the isolation would be more tolerable when at least two people shared the responsibilities.

As Tucson grew and more people began to move through the back country, there was less demand to keep the cabin staffed. Today fire crews may be temporarily stationed at the cabin. AlLong with reducing fuels and doing trail maintenance, they help monitor the threat of wildfire to the metropolitan area below.

1960 Fire Cabin at Happy Valley, now removed.

National Park Service

Hopi / National Park Service

Hopi Fire Tower, Grand Canyon NP

photo: Carol Young

Tower: Hopi
Year Built: 1953
Height: 23.5'
Manufacture: Baker Manufacturer modified
Model: L-4, 12 x 12 cab
Elevation: 7,140'
National Park: Grand Canyon, south rim
Access: Road
Rating: Inactive

Hopi Point, a rocky peninsula jutting into the vast space of the Grand Canyon, became popular as tourists began to flock to the Park in the early part of the century. Entrepreneurs, seeking tourism dollars, actively promoted trips to the canyon. From the railhead at Flagstaff, visitors traveled for days through the vast pine forests between Flagstaff and the south rim to peer into the depths of the Grand Canyon. By 1908, Park rangers were becoming concerned about the threat of wild fire due to the steadily increasing number of visitors. They built three fire towers, one at Hopi Point on the south rim two miles west of the El Tovar. A second was located at Bright Angel Point on the north rim and the third tower is at Pasture Wash, west of the Grand Canyon village. Kanabownitz was added later.

The original wood tower at Hopi Point was constructed in 1909, just four years after the Forest Service was founded in 1905. The original tower was a crow's nest with a ladder ascending the outside of the structure to an open platform surrounded by a railing. In 1913, the wood structure was replaced by a metal platform. In 1927, the Forest Service built a forty-three foot steel tower at a cost of $750., the cabin an additional $150. In 1952, the tower was struck by lightning and burned. It was replaced in 1953 by the current tower, just over twenty three feet high.

Along with Grandview fire tower, Hopi Point stood watch over the busy south rim into the 1990's when the increasing number of visitors reporting small fires reduced the need for a seasonal lookout at Hopi Point. Budget cuts made aerial reconnaissance seem more promising. The Park Service stopped manning Hopi Point.

The tower has not been dismantled. Signs around the perimeter warn visitors that this is private property and that vandalism will not be tolerated. In the mid 1990's, the structure was still used as a platform for monitoring air quality and storm observation. Otherwise, the Hopi Point tower has faded from public view. Today, visitors along the western rim, turn their eyes toward the canyon and fail to notice the narrow road that leads into the forest away from the rim, to a piece of our country's history.

Hopi

National Park Service

Kanabownitz / National Park Service

Tower:
Kanabownitz
Year Built: 1940
Height: 82.6'
Manufacture:
International Derrick
Model: 7 x 7 cab
Elevation: 8,241'
National Park:
 Grand Canyon,
  north rim
Access: Road
Rating: Inactive

Before the bridge was built across the Colorado River, the Bass trail was the main route across the canyon. Snowshoe Cabin, was built near the trailhead and used by rangers who patroled the district. Both the tower and the cabin made use of Kanabownitz Spring, one of the reasons the site was chosen for the two structures. The tower is located east of Shinumo Ampitheatre.

Kanabownitz

The Kanabownitz tower stands above the Point Sublime Road, overlooking an intricate network of canyons and ridges. To venture onto the Point Sublime Road requires an intrepid spirit along with good tires and a high clearance vehicle with four-wheel drive. At times the ruts threaten to high center the axles of one's vehicle. The trees close out the light, creating a netherworld of deep gloom on a cloudy day. On one short hill, the potholes threaten to swallow the entire wheel of our vehicle. Within a few miles we eagerly looked for some sign of civilization, a road marker or a landmark that would tell us our progress along the dirt track. The odometer seemed to snag on each tick as it slowly crept through the miles. It is a slow-going passage in a dark forest with lovely glens and wind swept meadows, deep forest gloom and moist canyons.

As our odometer ticked off the last tenth of a mile, confusion reigned. The tower was supposed to be to the right but no access road seemed to exist even as we drove on for another two miles only to turn back and look once again. We explored the ridge below Snowshoe Cabin, wondering if we had misunderstood. Was it only a cabin that had once harbored a ranger on horseback? As we turned back onto the Point Sublime Road, we caught a glimpse through drooping aspen of a dirt track. It was easy to miss. With the danger of vandalism, maybe the Park Service prefers to leave it that way. We followed the road on foot, climbing to the summit where we found the tower with solar panels in good repair. I knew this was not an active tower but it seemed as if the lookout had just stepped down for a moment and would return shortly.

When the tower was built in 1940 by the CCC, material costs were listed as $1,360.00 from the International Stacy (Derrick) Company. The materials were shipped to the railhead at Flagstaff and transported to the north rim. The tower was completed in October just before winter weather would have made access difficult. Labor cost were $500.00.

Without a doubt, Kanabownitz is one of the loneliest towers in the State due to the long, rough access and the lack of traffic long the road. We emerged with relief from the Point Sublime Road onto the well maintained roads of the North Kaibab National Forest.

National Park Service

North Rim / National Park Service

The North Rim tower once stood at Bright Angel Point. In 1934, the tower was dismantled and moved by the CCC to its current location, east of the north rim entrance station. The original tower had a ladder up the outside. In 1933, a new stairway was built up the center of the tower though the last flight remains a ladder through the trapdoor.

Due to the terrain, the tower is only marginally useful in its curent setting. The region has been called an inverted bowl, criscrossed by ridges. Edward Abby complained that the tower was placed 32 degrees off true north. Original cost of the tower was $952.48.

Tower:	North Rim
Year Built:	1933
Height:	75'
Manufacture:	Aermotor LX-24, mod.
Model:	7 x 7 cab
Elevation:	9,165'
National Park:	Grand Canyon, north rim
Access:	Road
Rating:	Inactive

*The Best of Edward Abby, a collection of Edward Abby's previous work, edited by Edward Abby. Publisher/ Sierra Club Books in conjunction with Crown Publishers, New York, NY. Copyright/ 1984

The North Rim has the notoriety of being one of the towers used by Edward Abby, noted environmental writer and fire lookout. It stands above State Route 64, rarely visited and even more rarely used. A dilapidated cabin, stands near the tower, its ceiling supported by improvised aspen trunks. Now missing a door and windows, the cabin was once the home of the lookout. But let Abby describe the tower as he once saw it.

"My career as a fire lookout began by chance. Having injured my knee during the Vietnam War (skiing in Colorado), I was unable to resume my usual summer job as patrol ranger in a certain notorious Southwestern national park. I requested a desk job. The Chief Ranger thought I lacked the competence to handle government paper work. He offered me instead the only job in the Park which required less brains, he said, than janitor, garbage collector or Park Superintendent. He made me fire lookout on what is called the North Rim, a post so remote that there was little likelihood I'd either see or be seen by the traveling American public. An important consideration, he felt.

The lookout tower on the North Rim was sixty feet tall, surmounted by a little tin box six feet by six by seven. One entered through a trapdoor in the bottom. Inside was the fire finder - an azimuth and sighting device - fixed to a cabinet bolted to the floor. There was a high swivel chair with glass insulators, like those on a telephone line, mounted on the lower tips of the chair's four legs. In case of lightening. It was known as the electric chair. The actual operations of the fire lookout, quite simple, I have described elsewhere.

My home after working hours was an old cabin near the foot of the tower. The cabin was equipped with a double bed and a couple of steel folding cots, a wood-burning stove, table, shelves, cupboard, two chairs. I made a pleasant home, there under the pines and aspen, deep in the forest, serenaded by distant coyote cries, by poorwills, and sometimes by the song of the hermit thrush, loveliest of bird calls in the American West." *

North Rim

National Park Service

Signal Hill / National Park Service

Signal Hill   Photo: Grand Canyon NP Archives

Tower: Signal Hill
Year Built: 1929
Height: 35'
Manufacture: Aermotor LS-40
Model: 7 x 7 cab

Elevation: 6773'
National Park: Grand Canyon, south rim
Access: Road
Rating: Inactive

Signal Hill

Signal Hill, west of the Grand Canyon Village on the South Rim, has been used over the centuries by succeeding cultures who left their residue upon the same site. This is evident at Signal Hill as the fire tower stands in the center of an old pueblo's ruins. It is amazing, considering the current effort to preserve the past, to think that the Park Service would erect a fire tower on the site of a ruin but there it stands as if in witness to the value that succeeding cultures placed on the site. The ruin walls have fallen over, leaving a line of rocks to define the size and location of the pueblo. Former lookouts have used the rock to line paths, leaving little chance of learning more about the people that once populated the site. The history of Pasture Wash and Signal Hill fire tower remains with the white settlers that moved into the area long after the ancient culture had abandoned the site.

The tower pre-dates the CCC era, built during the late 1920's as the Park Service began to come to terms with the popularity of the Grand Canyon. As tourists crowded into the Park, the threat of fire increased. The 1920's had seen few catastropic fires but the Park Service planned for the inevitable in building the tower. By 1954, the tower required new windows and flooring. A memo from the superintendent to the regional supervisor also suggested extending the ladder on the tower. Since that renovation little has been done to maintain the tower. The ravages of climate as well as vandals have left their own mark on the facility.

Though it remains the tower for the western half of the Grand Canyon National Park, Signal Hill has not been used for a number of years as the Park Service has begun to rely on aerial reconnaissance and the reports received from visitors to the back country. The lower steps have been removed from the tower to insure that visitors will not climb the stucture. No decision has been made about the future of the tower or the facilities at Pasture Wash.

National Park Service

Sugar Loaf / National Park Service

Sugar Loaf Mountain is the highest point in the Chiricahua National Monument. From the summit, looking south, one can see the Turkey Creek Caldera and Barfoot Park as it stands above Rustler Park. To the west a section of grasslands stretching along State Route 186 toward the little town of Elfrida is just visible between the rocky peaks. Below the peak, a forest of volcanic hoodoos stand silently in tribute to the explosive past found in Turkey Creek Caldera.

Tower: Sugar Loaf
Year Built: 1936
Height: 3'
Manufacture: Nat'l Park Service / CCC
Model: L-4 house, 12 x 12 cab
Elevation: 7,310'
National Park: Chiricahua National Monument
Access: Trail
Rating: Active

Sugar Loaf

The Chiricahua National Monument, established in 1924, preserves the Wilderness of Rocks with its vast display of rock hoodoos, grottos and seasonal creeks. If a fire started among the rock monuments, it would be difficult to fight in the dense brush and steep terrain. Sugarloaf Lookout remains an essential part of the watch over the Wilderness of Rocks, dating back to 1934 when Fred Wynn, National Forest Supervisor, proposed a fire cabin on Sugar Loaf Peak that would dovetail with Barfoot Lookout to stand watch over much of the northern Chiricahua Range.

To construct the fire cabin along with campgrounds, a visitors center and an improved road to Massai Point, the Federal Government proposed using the Civilian Conservation Corps. The Monument's Visitors Center houses a tribute to the men of the CCC camp.

The fire cabin has a historic look with it four foot high rock walls, topped by nineteen aluminum frame windows. The original wood shingles have been replaced by tile shingles. A concrete cistern was built under the cabin, providing water to the hand pump mounted on the counter inside. A trapdoor leads to a basement underneath the hardwood floor. The fourteen-foot square lookout is designed to be lived in, furnished with a kitchen counter and a cot. An outhouse stands nearby. However, due to the short commute, lookouts generally hike in from the parking lot below each morning. The lookout is manned by volunteers or Park fire crews from May into July when summer rains bring lightening strikes. The watch is discontinued when summer rain begin to dampen the forest in mid July.

While visitors are more likely to hike the Echo Canyon and Wilderness of Rock trails to look at the rock hoodoos, some hike the peak to get a bird's-eye view of the Monument from above. The road up to Massai Point is one of the premier scenic drives in the state. The trail to the cabin, a mile in length, gives hikers a chance to breath some fresh air, stretch their legs and enjoy some beautiful scenery as well as gain a bit of history.

National Park Service

Former Towers
Bright Angel Point
Year Built: 1928
Height: 75'
Manufacture: Aermotor LX-24
Model: 7 x 7 cab
Elevation: 8,250'
National Park: Grand Canyon / North Rim
This tower was originally located near the old wooden water tanks above the campgrounds at the North Rim. The original tower cost $952.48 and included a seventy-five foot ladder up the outside of the structure. In 1934, it was dismantled, moved and re-assembled at a location west of the North Entrance station. The cost of moving the tower and cabin to its current site was listed in the archives as $2471.71.

Mica Mountain
Year Built: 1938
Height: 99.9'
Manufacture: Aermotor MC-40
Model: 7 x 7 cab
Elevation: 8,664'
National Park: Sahuaro National Monument East
The tower was removed piece by piece to Tucson in 1985. Current location unknown

The Civilian Conservation Corps

The Civilian Conservation Corps played a major role in building many of the fire towers in the history of the Forest Service. They came into existence at a pivotal point in history that allowed them to be very effective in their work on behalf of our country.

In 1929, the United States economy entered the Great Depression, effecting the lives of millions of men and women for over a decade. As the Depression deepened, thousands were thrown out of work. Unemployment reached twenty-five percent nationwide with some local areas much higher. Many young men, without much experience, were unable to find employment and drifted through the country, following rumors of jobs in distant locations.

As Franklin D. Roosevelt entered office, he proposed a wide array of changes that would alter our economy. Most were overturned within a year but the Emergency Civilian Work project and the Civilian Conservation Corp proved to be a lifesaver for many young men and their families. The CCC was tailored after the military, installing young men in army tents with a strict regimen to their daily schedules. By 1935, enrollment peaked at 502,000 men spread across 2,514 camps nationwide. Enrollees were required to be male, unmarried, 17 to 23 years of age and unemployed.

At first, enrollees were sent to Fort Bliss in Texas and then back to Fort Huachuca for conditioning and training programs. The CCC established a ten-percent rule. Ten percent of the men must come from the local area where the camp was established, ten percent of the men must be military veterans. The remaining eighty percent frequently came from back east, their first experience in the wilderness of the wide open west.

In Arizona and New Mexico, thirty seven camps were erected throughout national forests, in national parks and on native American reservations. Between 1933 and 1942, nearly 53,000 men worked in the CCC camps based in Arizona. It is uncertain whether this also included the Native American camps. In an arid region like Arizona, the campsites were based on their accessibility to a water source. Along with the central camps, smaller 'fly camps' were built to allow the men to be closer to large jobs. The camps, built by the Army, were laid out with military precision, the tents in rows with a mess tent and officers quarters nearby. While the facilities were built by the Army, the men worked under the Departments of Agriculture and the Interior. The men rose at 6:00 in the morning to the sound of an army bugle with time to complete housekeeping chores and calisthenics before breakfast. After breakfast they reported to work details by 8:00, working till 4:00 in the afternoon with an hour off for lunch. Before and after dinner, they had time to participate in sports or take classes to improve their education. Some men learned to read in the classes. Others wrote letters home or spent time in the camp library. Lights went out at 10:00 in the evening.

The enlisted men were paid $30.00 a month. They kept $5.00 while the remaining $25.00 was withheld to be sent home to the men's families. Often this made a big difference in how the families fared as the depression deepened. The archives at Chiricahua National Monument note that many of the young men were half starved when they first showed up for their term of service. Within the first two months many had gained 20 pounds of muscle through hard work and three meals a day. When their first six-month commitment was completed, they were allowed to sign up for an additional term.

I visited the Chiricahua National Monument and found a roll-call of enlistees by year for the CCC camp that constructed many of the roads and facilities in the Monument. Carefully checking each year's listing, I found my husband's father listed. He had often recalled the year he spent with the CCC. He described how he came from a family with nine children and there was little to eat at home. He was turned down for military service and so came to the CCC. The camp had been assigned to build the central road through the Park as well as campgrounds and the Visitors Center. My father-in-law spent several months with a surveyor, mapping the grounds of the Monument. They clambered over the huge rock formations. When Evert, holding the pole, disappeared from site, the surveyor would instruct him to set the pole on his shoulder and then added his height to the reading. Years later, Evert returned with his children to show them what he had helped accomplish at the Monument.

The accomplishments of the CCC, went far beyond recreational facilities. Their efforts restored many miles of poorly used land. In the 1800's and early 1900's, the Conservation movement had brought public attention to the mismanagement of both private and public lands. The westward expansion coupled with the Homestead Act, had not been kind to the vast expanse of the western United States. Grazing had stripped natural grassesfrom semi-arid terrain. Loggers had clear cut vast areas of forested lands with the unfilled expectation that they would naturally recover. Hillsides and creek beds throughout the west were severely eroded. President Roosevelt saw the opportunity to resolve two problems with one solution. He instituted the CCC to work in America's vast public lands, restoring the damage that had been inflicted on the landscape. In the process, they came to be known as "Roosevelt's tree army."

In Arizona, they built roads, planted trees and worked at soil conservation and flood control. The CCC restored the river banks along the Salt and Verde Rivers as well as meadows that had been severely eroded by poor grazing practices. In Arizona, the CCC's work is evident in a visit to many of our state and national parks where the Corp developed recreational areas with campgrounds and hiking trails. The work of the CCC is distinctive in the craftsmanship of the stonework shown throughout campgrounds and public buildings. Many of the young men who learned rock work from the masons took the experience with them into commercial opportunities.

Throughout the country, they helped build over 90,000 miles of roads, some of them through public parks with the route surveyed by CCC crews. Flood culverts were often first put in place by CCC work gangs. Old photos from the Chiricahua National Monument show crews blasting away hillsides and carving routes through spectacular scenery. Old photos from the National Park Service also show the work done in the Grand Canyon building trails and recreational facilities. This included some heavy blasting to create routes for the trails against sheer rock cliffs. Louis Purvis, in writing The Ace In The Hole: A Brief History of Company 818 of the Civilian Conservation Corps, describes the critical judgement required to protect men from rock slides after explosives destabilized the sheer rock cliffs along new trails built in the Grand Canyon.

Under the Forest Service, the CCC built 3,470 fire towers and laid 65,000 miles of telephone line that allowed the lookouts to communicate with their district offices. The Aermotor towers, distinct in appearance from later structures, date back to the CCC era. The CCC also helped educate the public in preventing forest fires and were pulled off work projects to help fight forest fires as needed.

The men of the CCC were well received in the communities near the camps. Flagstaff, in Northern Arizona, had a population of 4,000 when

200 enlistees were shipped to the camp at the base of Mount Eldon in what is now east Flagstaff. When the men arrived, they were shocked at how small and isolated the town was compared to their homes in Pennsylvania. They were often polite, appreciative of the services the towns offered and added new blood to the life of the community. One restaurant owner laughed about the reception of the men in Flagstaff, saying, "You bet they were appreciated. A whole bunch of local girls married those CCC fellas."

The CCC's impact on this country is without precedent in the history of public work projects. They endured difficult climate conditions and yet exceeded expectations, earning the praise of neighboring communities for their character and hard work. Through the work experience they gained, many went on to private industry and successful lives. They look back with pride at their time in the CCC, fondly recounting stories from the camps.

After ten years of public service, the CCC was disbanded in 1942. Many of the young men went on to serve in the Armed Forces when the U.S. entered World War II.

A Civilian Conservation Corps work crew.

Bureau of Land Management

Chapter 2

The Bureau of Land Management is responsible for the federally owned land in Arizona not under the auspices of the Forest Service or Park Service. The Agency manages 12.2 million acres in Arizona with seven field offices throughout the state. This includes a major portion of the strip of land between the Grand Canyon and Utah, known as the Arizona Strip. Within the Arizona Strip, 19,000 acres are considered timbered while 11.92 thousand acres are categorized as rangeland. The Parashant Wilderness Area covers 11,054,264 acres through Arizona and Utah, all protected by the federal government from wholesale development by private concerns.

Much of the strip remains desolate and uninhabited. Driving west from Fredonia, the landscape is a drab brown, covered with sage brush, not a tree in sight. Visitors dropping south from Fredonia, toward the Grand Canyon are rewarded with the green pines that cover Mount Trumbull. Further west the Grand Wash cliffs create an imposing barrier to travel. Volcanic rock cliffs, impervious to flames, would not seem too threatened by wildfire. Call the BLM in Arizona about fire towers and the caller is informed that the BLM has no towers in Arizona. This is incorrect. Two towers, such as they are, sit in the northwest corner of Arizona overlooking the Pachun Valley and the isolated wooded peaks along the Nevada border. The towers are under the management of BLM Utah. This accounts for the confusion in whether there are BLM towers in Arizona.

Bureau of Land Management

The Forest Service maintains three fire towers on the eastern edge of the Strip. These lookouts report any smoke they site on the eastern edges of BLM land. The BLM towers stand watch over the western edge. The two towers hardly resemble the commonly accepted appearance of a fire tower. They were built to meet the demands of their specific locations. The tower at Black Rock is manned each year. The structure at Whitney Pass may have outlived the purpose for which it was built and remains inactive. While most of the population of Arizona may have no idea that these structures exist, Black Rock is frequently visited by sightseers out of Nevada and remains an important part of fire management in the region.

37

Black Rock / Bureau of Land Management

Black Rock Fire Tower sits on the edge of an ancient volcanic caldera The wind sweeps up out of the caldera and over the tower. At forty miles per hour, the windows shake, at sixty the cement block building starts to sway.

Black Rock Fire Tower, Photo: Hal Hilburn

Tower: Black Mountain
Year Built: 1981
Height: 10'
Manufacture: Bureau of Land Management
Model: R-6 flat
Elevation: 7,375'
District: BLM / St. George, UT
Access: Road
Rating: Active

Over sixty, the lookout would rather not talk to anybody as he can't hear the traffic on the radio. And just possibly his mind is on the security of the bulding surrounding him.

The two-story fire tower has a 360 degree view that overlooks Lake Mead to the south, the east side of the Virgin Mountains to the west, into Utah on the north and the Mount Trumbull region to the east. The terrain is volcanic rock with alternating areas of grass. A mix of manzanita and snowberry add contrast to the hillsides. At 7,310 foot elevation, the peaks are populated with ponderosa pine, a nice grove crowding the road below the tower. On a clear day, the lookout can see faint columns of smoke as far as ninety-five miles away. On bad days, haze creeps in from California and Las Vegas, greatly diminishing the area of oversite. Smoke simply disappears into the haze. Low lying clouds and rain may also cut off the horizon.

The building has a catwalk on three sides with windows in the remaining wall overlooking a steep dropoff. A number of agencies rely on repeaters and microwave towers at the Black Rock site. While it is classified as a live-in tower, the building offers only a bunk, two map tables and a desk. Lookouts bring a one burner stove, ice chests for food storage and a five gallon water jug. Down the hill from the tower is a cabin for fire crews that contains a fully furnished kitchen, flushable toilets and showers. Mack Thomson, the lookout, notes that he prefers a solitary existence to the late nights of the young men on the fire crews. For a fire lookout, the day starts early.

His nearest neighbors, other than the fire crew, live at a small ranch two miles away. There are no other neighbors for thirty-five miles though on weekends he has his share of visitors, many by ATV from Mesquite and Saint George. Some come for the view, more than once.

The fires reported from Black Rock are predominantly grass and brush though they can climb into the forest on the surrounding peaks. Mack has even reported an apartment fire in North Las Vegas which sent up a column of thick black smoke clearly visible to the little tower on the far side of the Virgin Mountains.

Black Rock

Bureau of Land Mngmt.

Whitney Pass / Bureau of Land Management

Whitney Pass,   Photo: Dave Lorentz

Tower: Whitney Pass
Year Built: 1962
Height: 3'
Manufacture: Bureau of Land Management
Model: L-4 house modified
Elevation: 4,400'
District: BLM / St. George, UT
Access: Road
Rating: Semi-Active

Whitney Pass

Bureau of Land Mngmt.

Lookout Mack Thomson describes Whitney Pass as the lookout from hell.

Why?

"Because it is the lookout from hell."

He explains by saying the building is set on a volcanic bluff that radiates heat over the site. When temperatures reach 110 in nearby Mesquite, at Whitney Pass they climb to 120 degrees. There is no shade, just black rock, snakes and spiders.

The ranchers of the Pachun Valley, below Whitney Pass, are an independent lot. The BLM became concerned about one rancher who would start a fire each year with the intention of improving his range. They built the Whitney Pass structure to keep an eye on his activities. Eventually they convinced him to apply for a burn permit each year though he often started a few days before the date on the permit.

The lookout can see into the deep canyons below Black Rock tower and the region south of the Virgin Mountains. The site has not been manned for the last two years and vandals have broken windows in the block building, allowing the elements to creep indoors. Mack is a bit surprised at the vandalism, noting that he did not have visitors when living at the site. Travelers would stop on the road below the cement block building, peering up at the structure as if to ask, "What is that?' And then move on down the road without investigating further.

It is a primitive site with a vault toilet and a shower stall. Lookouts bring their own baling twine to hang a solar heated shower. There is no power and no propane. Lookouts must drive two and a half hours to reach their site of employment and seldom see another person during their time on site.

At one time, a lookout also sat at Mount Logan. He kept watch from his vehicle in a pullout on the dirt road that climbs the peak. Between the three posts, fires were easily triangulated by the spotters. Today Black Rock is the sole lookout over this isolated region. The Whitney Pass Tower might be used in emergencies but it was not put in service during one of the worst fire years in 2005.

Hualapai Reservation

Chapter 3

The Hualapai Reservation was established in 1883, centered around the tribal headquarters at Peach Springs. Like many of the reservations in Arizona, the initial impression for visitors is desert land. Those who have traveled north to the edge of the Grand Canyon and the lands of the Havasupai know that green forests cover part of the Hualapai reservation. The rolling hills and quiet valleys are seldom explored by other than tribal members.

The reservation covers one million acres and extends 108 miles along the western rim of the Grand Canyon and the Colorado River. The elevation dips to 1500 feet at the river and rises to 7,300 feet at Aubrey Cliffs. Many of the higher hills are covered with ponderosa pine while the lower elevations are pinyon and juniper country. Around Peach Springs, the lowest elevation on the reservation, grasslands and desert dominate the landscape. One tower stands watch over the forests of the Hualapai with two other sites serving lookouts without benefit of an actual tower. Manzanita, one of the sites, had a crow's nest for lookouts but this has been removed. The splintered remains of an old cabin still stand at the site.

The tribe did not have a forestry program before 1978 when the Prospect Valley fire swept over 6000 acres. After the fire, a forestry program was initiated and eventually tribal lands came under the National Fire Danger Rating System. Under the program, the tribe had the financial resources to hire and train fire crews. Today, personnel from the Bureau of Indian Affairs as well as the tribal Forestry Department actively manage the forest.

The Prospect Valley fire was a turning point for fire managers on the Hualapai reservation, bringing significant changes in management practices to the reservation lands. Despite the lessons learned, the Hualapai struggle to use their natural resources to benefit the tribal members. Commercial timber sales are sporadic as transportation costs leave profits from commercial logging sales marginal at best. The newest commercial endeavor involves building a glass observation deck out over the western Grand Canyon.

Thorton / Hualapai Reservation

Thornton is the only fire tower located on the Hualapai Reservation. Oral history credits the IECW with building Thornton tower though no written records have been found to confirm this. The Indian Emergency Civilian Work program, a branch of the Civilian Conservation Corp, established one of the earliest IECW camps near Frasier Wells, the site of the tower, in 1933. The program was active from 1933 to 1942.

Tower: Thornton
Year Built: 1945
Height: 82.6'
Manufacture:
Aermotor / Hualapai Tribe / CCC

Model: 7 x 7 cab
Elevation: 6,780'
Access: Road
Rating: Active

The IECW was important to the reservation as it provided employment with wages for the first time to tribal members and opened inaccessible areas on reservation land through the conservation projects. The program also helped move the tribe toward self-governance. The most active years, 1933 through 1937, saw as many as forty-six enrollees per quarter, including women. Many of the men brought their families with them, pitching tents at the camp. Families included up to seven children. The enrollees were paid $30.00 per month.

The hundred-foot tower overlooks the sparsely populated forests of the Hualapai Reservation along Route 18. To the north lies the Grand Canyon and the Supai Tribal Reservation in Havasupai Canyon, to the south Highway 66 as it passes through Peach Springs. The reservation averages ten fires a season, usually caused by lightening strikes.

Angie, the lookout at Thornton, recalls her father serving as a lookout at the tower when she was only four years old. At that time several cabins stood near the tower, forming a small community, mostly occupied during the summer. An old wooden tower, possibly fifty feet high, also remained nearby. Today, it has been removed and a large metal building stands near the tower as a base for fire crews.

Thornton tower has a seven foot cab with a steel floor. Renovations were completed on the tower around 1998 with new siding, steps and windows. Angie wonders about the steel floor in a lightening storm and points to a rubber mat as her only insulator against a strike. She says she descends before lightening reaches the vicinity of the tower.

Not all fires are caused by lightening. Bob Nichols, a former BIA employee, recalls one fire that started with a bit of ambition. "Ben Beecher was out one year, working with his cattle. As night set in, he and another Hualapai man built a campfire to attract female company. They hoped the women would be drawn to the fire. Unfortunately, the fire soon spread into the woodland and started a wild fire. Norman Imus, Hualapai fire tech, followed the incident with a letter informing Mr. Beecher that he 'could not set the woods on fire to attract female company'. It just wasn't to be done."

Thornton

Hualapai Reservation

Former Towers / Hualapai Reservation

Manzanita
Year Built: 1940's
Height: 20'
Manufacture: Hualapai Tribe
Model: crow's nest
Elevation: 7,294'
Tribal Authority: Hualapai

The crow's nest was an open platform with the ladder ascending outside the structure. The structure was removed several years ago due to termite damage. Currently no fire tower stands at the site though the hill top is still used for observation during high fire danger. The site has two comunication towers rising above the summit though a lookout would make observations at the ground level. It has a good view of the Prospect Valley which was the site of the largest fire on the Hualapai Reservation in 1978.

The broken remnants of the lookout cabin on Manzanita Peak.

Kaibab National Forest

Chapter 4

The Kaibab National Forest has the distinction of being split in two by the Grand Canyon, a gulf 6000 vertical feet deep and up to eighteen miles in width. The southern portion of the forest is divided again by state land, essentially leaving the Kaibab in three distinct sections. The entire Kaibab covers 1.6 million acres. Elevation ranges from 5,500 feet to 10,418 feet at the summit of Kendrick Peak. The Supervisors Office for such a wide-spread Forest is located in Williams in the southern third of the Forest.

The North Kaibab, on the north rim of the Grand Canyon, covers 5,500 square miles. It is characterized by lush green firs, aspen and ponderosa, covering a maze of canyons and ridge lines. This northern section is a haven for mule deer, drawing hunters to the region every fall. Three fire towers are located in the North Kaibab.

The region south of the Grand Canyon below the National Park is the Tusayan district. Along with the Williams District, the southern Kaibab covers 1,422 square miles. The forest of the southern Kaibab varies from ponderosa pine at the south rim to pinyon and juniper around Red Butte. Two fire towers stand watch within the boundaries of the Tusayan district.

The southern-most district, centered around Williams, is visually-dominated by Bill Williams Mountain and Kendrick Peak. Much of the forest in this district is part of the largest contiguous yellow pine forest in the world. It is bordered on the south by the Prescott National Forest and to the east by the Coconino National Forest. All three of these Forests share parts of the Sycamore Canyon Wilderness area. Part of the eastern border also touches the Navajo Army Depot. Five towers stand on the Williams district, one of these in cooperation with the Navajo Army Depot.

Historically, the Kaibab has the unique distinction of having been set aside as a game preserve by President Teddy Roosevelt in 1906, about the time that the Forest Service was created. In 1919, the Grand Canyon National Park was created with its boundaries carved from parts of the Kaibab.

Kaibab National Forest

Bill Williams / Kaibab National Forest - South

The drive up Bill Williams Mountain is beautiful with massive old trees and a graveled road that swings through hairpin turns overlooking spectacular views of the surrounding forest. I was amazed at the number of lakes to be seen in the forest below: Fence, Dogtown, Davenport, Santa Fe, Park and Cataract. The little ponds of the Williams Golf Course shimmered in the late afternoon light. Yet the small Aermotor cab was cold and the lookout frequently

The last flight of stairs on this narrow tower is a tight squeeze as visitors enter the cab. Notice the odd red structure at top, unique among Arizona Towers. It may have been part of a radio antenna at one time.

Tower: Bill Williams
Year Built: 1937
Height: 45.9'
Manufacture: Aermotor MC-39
Model: 7 x 7 cab

Elevation: 9,256'
District: Williams / Kaibab
Access: Road & Trail
Rating: Active

used the heater throughout the day. The wind is a constant roar outside the windows. It is not a comfortable place to sit eight to twelve hours a day, five days a week.

This particular lookout does not like his tower! Standing watch so close to a population center is hard on this retired anthropology professor, who describes himself as an old Finnish hermit. Too many people find their way to Bill Williams tower, disturbing his solitude. Eric Hill insists half of Montana and Idaho are populated by old Finish guys like him who aren't social. They like their isolation. But he is not about to turn over his job to some 'wanna be tower watcher'. In mimicry, he throws an elbow at the door and growls, "get outta here!"

As Eric stands watch, he reads a lot, pondering the issues of life, taking a turn as philosopher. He says the job must be addicting. Every season as he leaves the tower, he swears this will be the last year. As a new spring rolls around, he finds himself returning to the tower. He shrugs, "I don't need the money. I feel like I'm sitting on top of the world," and with a smile, "I get to tell people where to go!" He notes that a select number of people do the job. They might not recognize each other in public but there is a sense of camaraderie that exists through the voices on the radio, the common effort to protect the land, the forest, the public.

Turning philosophical, Eric talks about making a contribution to society. "That's part of the problem with the country today. People fail to take personal responsibility. They don't contribute to the commonweal."

He may complain about the number of visitors yet he enjoys helping reunite separated parties. Eric recalls the woman who was to meet her husband at the summit after he took a solitary turn along a trail through the woods. He had the car keys. Two hours later, the husband was 'found' and the couple reunited. As she turned to go, Eric reminded her that a set of keys for each person is a good plan any time they entered the woods.

I suggested that for someone who values his reputation as a hermit, Eric seems to enjoy interacting with people. He shrugged, adding, "We are never as others see us."

Bill Williams

Kaibab National Forest South

Grandview / Kaibab National Forest - South

The boundary between the Grand Canyon National Park and the Kaibab Forest Service is more than a line on the map. It defines a difference in the management of scarce resources. The National Park fire operations manager relies on aerial reconnaisance rather than tower lookouts. This leaves the Kaibab's Grandview as the only tower on the south rim of the Canyon.

The usefulness of the lookouts in today's forest has been argued for years. The Grandview lookout defends the money spent, saying the money saved through early detection pays for the lookouts. A report from a lookout can make an hour, even a day's, difference in responding to a fire in our arid

Tower: Grandview
Year Built: 1936
Height: 81'
Manufacture: Aermotor MC-39
Model: 7 x 7 cab
Elevation: 7,531'
District: Tusayan / Kaibab
Access: Road & Trail
Rating: Active

southwestern terrain. Like other lookouts, she believes aerial reconnaisance is more suitable in the Northwest due to different terrain and fuels. The aerial recon complements the lookouts on the ground.

The Grandview lookout has spent fourteen seasons on six towers and sees the job as part of wild land fire management. "The thinking on fire management has changed from thirty years ago," she says. "District management may allow a fire to burn, with the lookout warning crews of hot spots, a change in the wind and advising the crews as the fire moves into a different fuel type. An experienced lookout can be solid gold for the crews on the ground maintaining communication about what they observe. They won't report campfires, holding off the call on isolated smoke until they determine what is happening. A volunteer may not see all this as they first begin to work the district. It takes an experienced lookout to listen to a high volume of radio traffic and pick out the important details."

Along with their other duties, some rangers may expect their lookouts to educate visitors, becoming a public resource. The lookout notes that the Tusayan FMO doesn't expect that from their lookouts. While it is good to be a resource, their number one job is to be a lookout. There have been times when large tour buses have pulled into the parking lot at the base of the tower. It is a popular spot, located along the Arizona Trail. The lookout, if busy, may choose to close the tower rather than allow a number of people to troop though the tiny cab. I considered the steep flights of stairs, without fencing along the hand rails, and suggested that liability might also be an issue for a crowd of hard-riding, bus-happy tourists.

Hikers and tourists are not the only disruption in the fire watch. Of hunters who drop in to ask about spotting deer or elk, the lookout mildly inquires, "you do realize you're shooting my neighbors?" Yet as a practical person, she understands the hunt fills home freezers. After hearing several lookouts make similar comments, I would suggest that hunting deer might not be the hot topic of discussion when visiting a lookout.

Grand-view

Kaibab National Forest South

Kendrick / Kaibab National Forest - South

Kendrick Peak is very popular with a steady stream of people climbing the three trails to the summit each weekend. The runners, many of which do this weekly, tap the pole next to the lookout and head back down while the hikers may visit for a few minutes.

Photos: Cliff Lewis

The lower level of the tower is cement block with a fifteen foot square live-in cab mounted one flight up. The cab has two bunks, a four burner stove, small refrigerator and a table with the fire finder dominating the center of the cab. A catwalk surrounds the cab, allowing the lookout to walk the perimeter, looking across the dormant cinder cones that surround the peak. On a clear day visibility can stretch fifty miles in each direction. Visitors can catch a glimpse of the rim of the Grand Canyon to the north and Jerome hanging on the side of the Bradshaws far to the south. Clear days are rare.

There is no road to the summit of Kendrick. Supplies must be hauled in by foot or mule. In the spring the lookout may forge a route through four foot high drifts of snow if the winter has been harsh. Each week the lookout begins the climb to the summit with a pack full of groceries, clean clothes and supplies. They remain there for five days with a volunteer serving on weekends. Kendrick is one of three towers in the region that actively uses volunteers as relief.

In 2005, Roger and Kathy, married for thirty-five years, shared the responsibilities. Roger frequently took the hand radio and worked outside, studying the environment, piling rocks or other self-assigned chores. He was eager to show visitors all the attractions from 'fossil man' to a signal mirror which he used to signal fire crews, other lookouts or hikers on the trail. A hole in the middle of the mirror allowed him to aim the reflection of the sun at his target.

The couple related their experience in nursing, as a prison guard and as a geological engineer. That experience has stood them in good stead for the unusual visitors that dropped in at off moments. They recall men who have shown up on a dark night, dressed all in black on reconnaissance or the visitor who arrived on their catwalk at dawn before they had opened the door to the stairway below. Regardless of the unexpected visitors, they welcomed those who wandered through their bird's eye view of the world, answering the same questions repeatedly. As we made our way down the mountain, a spot of sunlight danced around us to the delight of the two young girls hiking with me. Roger was practicing his skills with the signal mirror. We waved and turned back to the trail, four miles downhill to the parking area.

Tower: Kendrick	Model:
Year Built: 1964	R-6 flat, 14 x 14 cab
Height: 10'	Elevation: 10,418'
Manufacture:	Access: Trail
USDA Forest Service CL100-106	Rating: Active

A half mile below the summit is a cabin that was once home to the lookout when a crow's nest stood on the peak. The cabin now serves as a hikers rest and historic site.

Kendrick

Kaibab National Forest South

Red Butte / Kaibab National Forest - South

I met my first volunteers, Jane and Skip, at Red Butte. They have been volunteering their weekends to sit on fire towers each summer for about ten years. They started volunteering as a way to get out of Phoenix on the weekends. Now they simply enjoy the quiet solitude. He is a nurse. She has been a teacher as well as working in other areas in education. Both have Masters degrees. When Skip returned to school for a nursing degree, he found that the time

Tower: Red Butte
Year Built: 1980
Height: 12'
Manufacture: USDA Forest Service CL 100-106
Model: R-6 duel cab with modified windows
Elevation: 7,324'
District: Tusayan / Kaibab
Access: Trail
Rating: Active

The current tower may have replaced two previous towers.

spent at the tower was good for studying, providing he could lug fifty pounds of books up the steep trail from the parking area below the tower. (The road is not open to visitors.)

When she isn't on the lookout, Jane may be stationed at the top of the Arizona Snowbowl Sky Ride where she talks to visitors about the awesome scenery at their feet as well as the fragile vegetation around them. She also helps write recreational guides and disability guides for the handicapped for the Forest Service.

Both regard a beautiful sunrise and sunset as one of the perks of the job. They also like working together on the weekends. They enjoy the songbirds that drop in for a visit on their migration routes each fall and spring. But their favorite visitors may be the covens of ravens that circle the tower. Some days as many as fifty to seventy ravens indulge in rolls and dives, playing in the wind currents that sweep the peak. Skip says that if a bird could smile, the ravens are smiling in their aerial acrobatics.

They talked about the fires they have seen on the job, including the recent Muderback fire. They could see the flames leaping above the landscape as the fire was allowed to burn under control. They mentioned the spectacular lightning shows with strikes 360 degrees around the tower. They talked about the trail washing out during heavy rains. It is a unique way to spend a weekend.

Red Butte is one of the more secluded locations for a lookout seeking a spot off the beaten track. It requires visitors to hike a mile and a half to reach the tower. Jane and Skip are the weekend subs for the full time lookout, Bruce Hill. Bruce is a well known artist, painting southwestern landscapes in beautiful pastels. He takes much of his inspiration from the landscape surrounding the tower. Visitors may catch a glimpse of a rain storm moving across the arid landscape, captured on canvas, leaning against the wall of the tower.

Not all towers are open to volunteers. Schedules vary. On Kendrick, the full time lookout works five days a week with volunteers on the weekends where as on Red Butte, the schedule is split ten on, four days off.

Red Butte

Kaibab National Forest South

Red Hill / Kaibab National Forest - South

Tower: Red Hill
Year Built: 1958
Height: 10'
Manufacture: USDA Forest Service CL 100-106
Model: R-6 Duel Cab
Elevation: 7,751'
District: Chalender / Kaibab
Access: Road
Rating: Inactive

Red Hill

The forests of the Williams district drop from ponderosa pine into the pinon and juniper. The sap-fragrant pines of the transition zone are slow to ignite but once burning create a fierce fire. A number of cinder cones, including Red Hill, rise out of the juniper, north of Parks. Red Hill is not as well known as Red Mountain, and this may be a good thing for fire watch as the lookouts are seldom disturbed The tower, accessed by a road that circles the low peak, is no longer manned on a regular basis since the last regular lookout retired. If a hot, dry summer arrives with fiery lightening storms, a watch may be set for a few days. It would seem a prime location for a volunteer when neighboring Red Butte and Kendrick are manned every weekend with volunteers.

The cab, set on a ten-foot high cinder block base, offers a wide open view to the north of Red Butte, Red Mountain and State Route 64. The southern exposure overlooks the San Francisco Peaks, Kendrick Peak and Bill Williams Mountain. The view of nearby Slate Mountain gives new respect for this often ignored peak.

Nearby Kendrick Peak has been the site of two fierce fires in the last few years, giving Red Hill a front row seat in the fight to save the densely forested peak. The tower is a prime site to watch the small communities springing up north of Williams and Parks, all at risk in a tinder dry forest where flames would build quickly.

The tower has become the haunt of pack rats who use it to stash juniper berries. The upper story of the tower has room for a bunk and kitchen counter around the central fire finder. A hand pump dominates the counter though whether it still gives water is questionable. A water reservoir sits on the north side of the building.

Just below the water reservoir, the cement foundation of an old cabin is visible along a rocky shelf. Cement stairs lead down to the foundation indicating that it must have been a cabin or storage facility. A flagpole stands nearby. The tower was heavily vandalized several years ago. It has since been repaired and the Forest Service hopes to maintain the facility in good condition.

Kaibab National Forest South

Round Mountain / Kaibab Nat'l Forest - South

Tower: Round Mountain
Year Built: 1955-1960
Height: 35'
Manufacture: Aermotor MC-39

Model: 7 x 7 cab
Elevation: 7,214'
District: Williams / Kaibab
Access: Road
Rating: Inactive

Dogtown and White Horse Lake are two of the most popular recreation areas in the southern Kaibab National Forest, drawing a large number of visitors. Along with the two lakes, Sycamore Canyon is a dominant feature in the Kaibab, presenting a formidable challenge for fire fighters if a fire should break out in the isolated canyon. Bill Williams Tower surveys much of this region but little Round Mountain still reserves the best views of White Horse Lake and the northern end of Sycamore Canyon.

The current tower dates to the late 1950's and has not been used in recent years. In a very dry year, the fire manager may send a lookout to the site for a few hours, particularly if the Forest has been closed. Fire crews may also use the tower to check the location of a smoke report.

The access is rough with the surface of FR138 a maze of deep ruts and protruding rocks that must be carefully negotiated. The tower sits in a small clearing at the summit of Round Mountain. It is a unique MC-39 Aermotor, modified so that the stairs lead to a small platform on one side of the seven foot square foot cab rather than entering through a trap door in the floor. The tower remains as a resource for dry years, rather than being dismantled.

Round Mtn.

Kaibab National Forest South

Volunteer / Kaibab National Forest - South

Volunteer Fire Tower is the only fire tower located on a military base in Arizona. Visitors must obtain permission from the commander of the Navajo Army Depot to drive up to the tower. The lookout notes that this is the biggest difference between his tower and others on the Forest. He does not have visitors except as requested from base personnel. His wife or grandson

Tower: Volunteer	Model: R-6 flat, 14 x 14 cab
Year Built: 1963	Elevation: 8,047'
Height: 30'	District: Chalender / Kaibab
Manufacture:	Access: Road
USDA Forest Service CL 100-106	Rating: Active

may accompany him for the day but otherwise it is a very quiet on Volunteer Peak. He appreciates the cell phone and forest service radio that allow him contact with civilization.

Volunteer Fire Tower sits on the boundary between the Coconino and Kaibab National Forest. Though the immediate vicinity is under military control, the horizons are Forest Service lands. The lookout must know his landmarks and his maps to determine which Forest beyond NAD boundaries is notified of a fire. Of the three towers on the Williams district, Bill Williams and Kendrick are considered the primary and secondary towers. However, Volunteer completes a triangle with the other two, overlooking areas that are blocked from the view of the other two towers by hills or ridges.

Along with the NAD, his primary areas of observation are Parks and Garland Prairie, both of which are populated with isolated homes each built on two or more acres. Garland Prairie is highly susceptible to grassland fires. The lookout recalled one lightning strike that sparked a snag. The flames spread through the tall grass to another snag, rapidly moving forward till the blaze covered nine acres.

The current tower, in service during WWII, replaced a wood structure built in 1932. In the early years, Volunteer was manned by NAD personnel. Restored by the NAD, Volunteer is a well maintained tower with a refrigerator, stove, counter and sink with running water, a bunk and a large map table surrounding the fire finder. Below the tower is a two room cabin that was once used as a residence for the lookout. The tower is currently uninhabitable except by four-legged residents. The tower is surrounded by communications towers, some private, some military.

Before his service as a lookout, Mr. Olson flew for the Forest Service as well as for three private tour companies in Tusayan south of the Grand Canyon. His missions included dropping fire retardant on fires and transporting fire crews into sites inaccessible from the ground. He flew the S55T Sikorskys, also known as pregnant guppies for their large cargo compartments on the belly of the aircraft. After flying helicopters under such demanding circumstances, his time in the tower is very quiet.

Volunteer

Kaibab National Forest South

Big Springs / Kaibab National Forest - North

Imagine raising your family each summer on a hundred foot fire tower with open stairs and active children. Big Springs is known as the family tower. Ross took up the watch when his mother retired after fifty two years of service at Dry Park and Big Springs. He recalls climbing the stairs as a child, to find his mother at work with the fire finder and the binoculars. Each summer the family packed up seven kids to spend a few months in a one-room cabin in the meadows and tall pines above Big Springs. Their light came from gas propane lanterns. Water was hauled from the spring at the bottom of the ridge. He does not recall being bored but relates the simple games they invented using the structure as a staging ground. In one such game, they would begin with the first flight, dropping rocks down the center well. Once completed, they would climb to the next level and the next, trying to be the one who successfully dropped rocks from each level without touching metal.

Tower: Big Springs
Year Built: 1934
Height: 100'
Manufacture: Aermotor MC-39
Model: 7 x 7 cab
Elevation: 7900'
District: North Kaibab, Kaibab N.F.
Rating: Active

He recalls his one year old brother climbing the tower. They caught him half way up but allowed him to climb with an escort close behind, ready to scoop him up at the slightest stumble. The following day, his father installed a gate at the base of the stairs to prevent any further excursions.

One summer Ross kept a cage of ten to twelve chipmunks as pets and remembers the excitement when they escaped their prison inside the little cabin. It took days before all the creatures were chased from the cabin and peace reigned once again. An army of their descendants still roam the stairs and foundation of the cabin below. As he grew older his exploits became more daring. He recalls climbing out the window of the tower cab and making his way along the steel struts to the ground with his best friend on a mutual dare. As I gazed at the distance between the struts, I cannot imagine how they stretched for each handhold. Another adventure involved hiking the canyon rim to rim, camping and fishing, climbing the last miles in the moonlight to catch a ride the last few miles to the cabin with the mailman.

As an adult he worked the river one year, then two years at Zion National Park. His first teaching job was in Moccasin, just a bit north of the Rim. After a career in teaching, he moved houses. When he retired, he returned to Big Springs fire tower. At night he hears the screams of mountain lions that have wandered near the tower. Most human visitors who find their way to his little meadow are a bit lost and quite surprised to find him in a tower at the end of the road. He freely gives out directions to their next destination.

As we talked, humming birds darted around the windows, sipping a bit of nectar, battling for control of the feeding space. He once hung a bottle inside the tower and "OH MY!" The speed of the birds zipping through the enclosed space around his head was a bit much. It was the only day a bottle hung inside the tower.

His view from the tower includes Kanab and Kanab Canyon, Zion and Bryce National Parks, Pine Mountain and the little town of Moccasin where his mother resides as the "tower lady". Unlike his mother, he doesn't see himself doing this till age eighty.

Big Springs

Kaibab National Forest North

Dry Park / Kaibab National Forest - North

Tower: Dry Park
Year Built: 1944
Height: 120'
Manufacture: Aermotor MC-99

Model: 7 x 7 cab
Elevation: 8708'
District: North Kaibab / Kaibab
Access: Road
Rating: Active

To visitors, Dry Park Tower, at a hundred twenty feet, seems to pierce the sky. Set foot on the first step and the stairs sway in a gentle rocking motion as visitors ascend the first two flights. It is a little unsettling. Yet, the tower is solid, each flight strung between the four supports, steadily narrowing as it gains height. However, when the wind rises to thirty miles per hour, visitors at the top may note that the trees outside the tower appear to move from one window to the next. It certainly gives visitors pause about how high they have climbed.

There was a little competition between Dry Park and Chediski over who would claim the honor as highest tower in the state. Those who built Chediski, added an extra three inches to the cement base, hoping to claim that honor. While Chediski is in a restricted area of the White Mountain Apache reservation, Dy Park is accessible to any who take the time to search out the location along the rocky roads of the north rim of the Grand Canyon. Despite its easy access, the tower can be a lonely site. Just two days before we visited the Dry Park tower, the watch signed off for the last time that season. He told his fellow lookout in Big Springs that he just couldn't take the loneliness any longer. And so the tower stood empty during the latter half of the 2005 fire season.

Dry Park covers the region between the Grand Canyon National Park to the south, Big Springs to the north, DeMotte Park and a state highway on the east. and Kanab Canyon to the west. Only a few visitors find their way down the side route off SR 67 to the base of one of the tallest towers in the state. Even fewer find the nerve to climb the structure though it seems more secure than some of the smaller towers on other Forests. Besides battling for budget dollars, keeping qualified people in the towers may be one of the biggest challenges for fire tower managers in the more remote areas of the state.

It is a beautiful site with a meadow of wild flowers that doubles as a helipad. At the base of the tower, a well kept two room cabin offers a home to the lookout. A weather station and water tower sit along the edge of the meadow.

Dry Park

Kaibab National Forest North

65

Jacobs Lake / Kaibab National Forest - North

Why did Mark Gurmon take the job as lookout on a hundred foot tower? To get over his fear of heights! At last I had found a kindred spirit!

The Jacob's Lake tower is located just off SR 67, the main route to the north rim of the Grand Canyon. Even with the prominent location, Mark only sees on average fourteen visitors a day. The height of the tower and

Tower:
  Jacob Lake
Year Built:
  1934
Height: 100'
Manufacture:
  Aermotor
    MC-39
Model:
  7 x 7 cab
Elevation:
  8161'
District:
  North Kaibab,
    Kaibab N.F.
Access: Road
Rating: Active

the narrow, open stairs deter some would be visitors. Some freeze half-way up the ascent, close their eyes and cautiously back down the stairs. Mark samples each contact like a gift, happy to shake hands and get to know his visitors.

Some visitors take note of an old broom hanging by two hooks from the ceiling. It looks much like the broom from the popular series of Harry Potter movies. Invariably they ask, "So, you use it to fly down from the tower?" As if a guy with a fear of heights would fly a broom! Instead he races down the flights of steps, eager to show the confidence he has acquired in his time on the tower.

Mark credits the tower with the best views of Utah, noting the brilliant red cliffs on the northern horizon. His southern horizon is a ridge that blocks the view of the Grand Canyon, a challenge in reporting the distance and elevation of fire locations. Mark proudly keeps a record of those fires that he reports accurately. He hears little bleed-over on channels with the Utah-based fire agencies but during a fire he may be asked to change channels until the fire is under control. Along with spotting fires, Mark has a bird's eye view as the Highway Patrol stops speeders along SR 67 below his perch.

He recalls his first year in the tower - no training, simply a map with a radio. If he didn't quite get it right, the other lookouts as well as his boss graciously guided him along.

Jacobs Lake is one of two staging areas on the north rim for fighting wildfire. In 2004, all but three of the fires on the North Rim were caused by lightning strikes. The tower has been struck twice by lightning. The most memorable included a strike directly overhead followed by a second strike to the side of the tower where he was sitting. Mark woke up five minutes later on the floor of the cab, his head a little fuzzy about the details of what had just happened. He credits District management with putting safety first for their lookouts whether lightning strikes or maintenance on the tower.

We leaned over the edge of the window, two vertically challenged adults, to examine the historic markings on the side of the cab. The dates were left by lookouts from the 1930's and 1940's. It gives a sense of perspective to the tower, the watch and the sea of green spreading across the horizon.

Jacobs Lake

Kaibab National Forest North

Tree Towers of the Kaibab

Installing a ladder on a lookout tree.
Photo: Grand Canyon National Park Archives

Tree Towers of the Kaibab

Before the fire towers were built, forest rangers would climb tall trees on a hill top or ridge to look for a plume of smoke rising above the forest. In time, they began to build ladders up specific trees at prime locations and return to these ladders on a regular patrol. The trees became known as "lookout trees." Some of the lookout trees remain today with the remnants of ladders or stairs ascending through the branches to a breath-stealing height. Other trees have lag bolts pounded into the trunk of the tree, taking the place of a ladder. Those who have climbed the lag bolts describe the experience as requiring a little less common sense than that of the average man.

In the 1930's many of the tree towers were initially built by the Civilian Conservation Corp. In his book describing his days in the CCC, Louis Purvis recalls one black smith, a Mr. George Shields, who constructed many of the iron ladders that were attached to the lookout trees. The ladders were built in sections at his blacksmith shop and then transported to the specific trees where they were attached by lag bolts. In old records, materials acquisitioned to construct one of the ladders were listed as: 1200 feet of random lengths of angle iron sized 1.25 x 1.25 x .125 inches, 600 feet of .75 x .75 x .125 iron. To assemble the lengths, 1300 3/8" x .75" round head rivets and 400 .5 x 4" lag screws were ordered. The cost of the ladders ran between $100 and $200.

The rungs of the ladders, made from three quarter inch angle iron, were spaced between thirteen and sixteen inches apart, the ladders about thirteen inches wide. Some lookout trees contained an actual platform either built across the branches or the top of the tree was lopped off and the platform constructed across what remained of the main trunk. On some trees, the ladder simply ascended through the branches and the lookout was maintained from a solid branch many feet above the ground. If a platform existed, there was usually a railing around the top as a safety feature for the men on watch. A heavy copper wire ran from the top of the tree to the ground to serve as a conductor should lightning strike the tree.

Kaibab National Forest

Building the ladders. Photo: Grand Canyon Nat'l. Park Archives.

The terrain of the North Kaibab National Forest made lookout trees particularly useful to the fire crews that patrolled this region. The terrain is a maze of ridges and deep canyons, inverted bowls and dense forests. Only two fire towers currently exist along the North Rim of the Canyon and three towers on the north Kaibab. The lookouts' observation of the region is limited due to the terrain. It was easier and less expensive to attach ladders to a lookout tree in prime locations rather than to build and maintain a fire tower.

As the years have passed and the trees that remain have grown in height and circumference, some have engulfed their ladders, making the climb a bit risky. Dr. Dave Lorentz, an authority on Arizona's fire towers, has described climbing one tree to find the tree bark having grown around the rungs about eighty feet above the ground. As he clung to the ladder, he noted his precarious position. He knew if he should fall and be injured, it would be a long time before he was rescued as the area was seldom visited. He carefully descended the ladder, deciding discretion was the better part of valor in his zeal to maintain the public record. He has recorded the location of each of these trees for the Forest Service but the exact locations have not been made public. Visitors are not actively encouraged to visit the sites unless they express a specific interest in the history of lookout trees. Many of the people who have visited one of these trees have stumbled across them by accident.

The following is a partial list of lookout trees on the North Kaibab and the North Rim of the Grand Canyon. The list includes the height of their observation points along with the elevation of their location.

North Kaibab & North Rim Lookout Trees:

North Rim	82.6
Bright Angel Point Tree	100'3" @ 8250'
Swamp Ridge Tree	109' @ 8,300'
Kanabowntiz Tree	98' @ 8250'
Sublime Ridge Tree	90'2"@ 8,000'
Pond Canyon Tree	96'4" @ 8400'
Neal Ridge Tree	98'6" @ 8660'
Lindberg Hill Tree	86'6" @ 8780'
Two River Junction Tree	83'3" @ 8500'
Nankoweap Tree	96'8" @ 8800'
Outlet Ridge Tree	101'7" @ 8300'
Tiyo Ridge Tree	100'8" @ 8300'
Fire Point Tree	85' @ 7980'
Walhalla Tree	no further information
Long Jim Canyon	70' @ 7000'
Grapevine	85' @ 7400'
Shoskey Jct.	80' @ 6800'
Hermit	30' @ 6700'
Duck on Rock	28' @ 7250'

The trees are marked with a small tag labeled TT followed by the number of the tree. If visitors stumble across a tree with protruding lag bolts or a ladder that ascends into the branches, Dave highly recommends looking but not climbing the ladder. Often these ladders have deteriorated and are hazardous. Instead, take a moment to appreciate a glimpse back into the history of fire prevention and forest preservation without risk to property or one's well being.

Former Towers /Kaibab National Forest

Skinner Ridge
Year Built: 1929
Height: 60'
Manufacture: Aermotor Mc-39
Model: 7 x 7 cab
Elevation: 7,248"
District: Tusayan

Summit Mountain
Year Built: 1916/1919
Height: 30'
Manufacture: Forest Service
Model: Tree Tower
Elevation: 7,797'
District: Williams

Dave Lorentz cites a Superintendent's Report, saying the Rowe Ranger Station was once considered as a site for a sixty foot Aermotor tower. The site offered a good view to the south and west of the Grand Canyon. While there is no record that the tower was built, a tree tower is near the site.

A working water pump stands on the catwalk of the thirty foot Apache Maid fire tower on the Coconino Natinal Forest. It saves the lookout multiple trips up and down the stairs hauling water for daily use.

Coconino National Forest

Chapter 5

The Coconino National Forest spreads over 1,821,495 acres in north central Arizona. Elevation ranges from 2,600 feet in the southwestern corner to 12,633 feet at the summit of Mount Humphreys. The ponderosa pine of the Coconino are part of the largest contingous yellow pine forest world-wide, covering a 7,000 foot high plateau cut by deep canyons lined with red sandstone.

The Coconino is managed through four ranger districts. The region around Flagstaff is divided between the Peaks and Mormon Lake Ranger districts. The Peaks Ranger district is an ancient hot spot with dormant cinder cones rising above the ponderosa pine forest. The Mormon Lake district extends along a high mesa dotted with small lakes and open green meadows.

The Mogollon Rim district is named after a 2,000 foot high escarpment that stretches across the Coconino from Flagstaff into the Sitgreaves National Forest. The rim receives a lot of moisture allowing dense forest to blunt the severity of deep canyons that drop over a thousand feet toward the Tonto National Forest. The Red Rock Ranger district lies along the southernwestern edge of the Coconino, bordering the Prescott National Forest. Both the Prescott and Coconino Forests are responsible for large tracts of land within the Verde Valley.

Along with the Apache Sitgreaves, the Coconino sees a large number of visitors from the southern deserts who come to enjoy the green, cool mountains of northern Arizona. The yellow pine forest so valued by northern residents of the state leaves the region a prime candidate for wildfire, either at the hands of the public or by lightening strikes during the summer rains.

Twelve fire towers stand watch over the Coconino. These include the only two wooden towers in the state. Seven other sites have been identified as a base for other towers that have since been dismantled and removed. All but one of the remaining towers are in active service. Mormon Lake tower is no longer used. It still stands but the stairs have been removed.

Coconino National Forest

Apache Maid / Coconino National Forest

Tower: Apache Maid
Year Built: 1961
Height: 30'
Manufacture: USDA Forest Service CL100-106
Model: R-6 flat, 12 x 12 cab
Elevation: 7,301'
District: Verde Valley / Coconino
Access: Road
Rating: Active

This tower may be one of the most unique in Arizona, not for its design, but in how multiple agencies cooperated in the construction of the tower and the field work surrounding the site. It was built in 1962 as part of the Beaver Creek Watershed Study at a cost of $5980. An additional $2,020. was spent on a latrine (400.), cabinets and furnishings (750.), a water supply with tank and system (1000.), a utility building (500.) and flag pole (100).

Apache Maid

Coconino National Forest

The lookout on Apache Maid calls his position a good job after spending years on the back of a horse, trailing cows and building fences in Bloody Basin. In a quiet drawl, James notes that there are no pensions for 'cowpunchers' and he still likes to eat. Yet those years as a cowpuncher come to good use as he knows the terrain below his feet, the same ground he now observes from the Apache Maid tower. But names can be deceiving. When he showed up for a meeting of lookouts on the Coconino, another lookout came up and said he wanted to meet the fellow who identified himself as an "Apache Maid!"

Apache Maid fire tower surveys a terrain with mostly pinyon and juniper scattered through extensive grasslands. The higher elevations are covered with ponderosa pine. The most prominent feature slashing across the southern horizon are the vertical cliffs of Wet Beaver Creek. Along the northern horizon, the upper edge of the depression surrounding Stoneman Lake is just visible. In the meadows below the tower is Discovery Camp, a refuge for troubled boys. They come to visit occasionally, hiking up the little peak to the tower.

To the west, I-17 presents a major challenge to the Apache Maid lookout with all the traffic moving between Phoenix and the high country. The two months before the summer rains arrive are the most active time with vehicle fires, people tossing cigarettes out of cars, sparks from catalytic converters, flat tires on a trailer or a truck may blow a compressor. All of these incidents blow hot sparks into the dry tinder lining the interstate and soon a call comes in from Apache Maid, reporting yet another fire. His duties may also involve serving as a relay between the Coconino and Prescott National Forests and their mobile units.

James calls the new radio system one of his biggest challenges as it is based on a narrow band. He notes that the voices may fade but the static always comes in loud and clear. Both the base and handheld unit run on power from solar panels. Each day as the sun reaches its highest point or equinox, the radio runs out of power and then comes back to life as the sun begins its descent. For a few minutes, the tower is very quiet.

Baker Butte / Coconino National Forest

Shirley Payne started her career as a lookout out at Moqui. The first day, in seventy mile per hour winds, she made her way up the stairs, clutching two children by their tiny hands, with a one-year-old baby in a pack, hanging from her shoulders. With each flight of stairs she asked what she had gotten herself into as she maintained her death grip on the children. She had not received much training and lived in fear that someone would call her when the baby would be crying and that the cries would blast out over the radio. She worked on Moqui for twelve years before the FMO asked her to switch over to Baker Butte. Twenty one years later, her children are grown and as a well-seasoned lookout she continues her watch.

Tower: Baker Butte
Year Built: 1937
Height: 30'
Manufacture:
    Aermotor MC-24

Model: L-4, 12 x 12 cab
Elevation: 8,074
District: Blue Ridge /
    Mogollon Rim / Coconino
Rating: Active

From her tower, on a clear day, she can see north to the San Francisco Peaks above Flagstaff or as far south as Mt. Lemmon towering above Tucson. Her region includes the forest along the Mogollon Rim, Four Peaks, the Sierra Anchas and the Supersition mountain ranges as well as the populated areas around Payson.

As we talked about the visible landmarks, she pointed to a plume of smoke rising near Bull Run and told me she called it in the previous day. No one had been assigned to work it. Over the next hour, the column of smoke continued to grow. She gave one of the fire management technicians an update by radio on the smoke. He told her they are allowing it to burn.

As she talked to the tech, I examined the post cards that lined the walls of her tower. She received her first card from a professor at the University of Arizona. After visiting the tower one summer, he sent her a card while on a trip to Russia. Soon other visitors began to send her cards, some from other towns in Arizona, many from around the world. As they filled the upper reaches of the tower, she began to tack them onto the walls of the cabin at the base of the tower.

The cabin was originally one room till two additional rooms were hauled to the site. The cabin reflects Shirley's interests, the kitchen stuffed with baking supplies, beautiful quilts covering the bed and furniture. Over the winter, thieves broke into the cabin and stole a portable washing machine and a lucky dollar.

As we talked, a work crew on SR 87, below the tower, called Shirley on the radio. "Shirley, can you get dispatch to call a tow truck for a stranded party down here? We can't get through to them on the radio." She picked up her cell phone to avoid putting the request out over the entire district. After parlaying between road crew and dispatch, she pulled out a sheet of cardboard covered with phone numbers and called the tow truck.

We briefly discussed aerial recon and she asked a pertinent question. "What are we here for?" Shirley does a lot of relay traffic for the mobile units. I think about the stranded motorist. The lookouts are much more than fire spotters.

Baker Butte

Coconino National Forest

Buck Mountain / Coconino National Forest

Tower: Buck Mountain
Year Built: 1939
Height: 30'
Manufacture: USDA-FS
Model: CT-2 wood,
          12 x 12 cab
Elevation: 7,571'
District: Long Valley
  Mogollon Rim / Coconino
Access: Road & Trail
Rating: Active

Why Wood?
Why build a tower out of wood, a flammable material? Note that the tower was built in 1943, during World War II. Steel was scarce, with all metals directed to the war effort. The Forest Service returned to steel towers after the war years. East Pocket and Buck Mountain are the only two wooden towers remaining in Arizona.

The Buck Mountain Fire Tower was constructed in 1939 by the Civilian Conservation Corp. After years of service, the wood structure began to deteriorate. The tower, listed on the Historic Register, was a liability to the Coconino Forest Service. Funds were allocated to restore the structure and it is now a show piece in historic reconstruction for the district. The reconstruction was completed in 2003 when the cab, the catwalk and the stairway were completely replaced, using materials in compliance with the historical restoration and construction methods from earlier decades. The tower structure and the roof remained in good condition.

    To climb the wood stairs is to climb into history, imagining a lithe figure in green and brown with a Smokey Bear hat planted firmly on his head, climbing this same structure in the early days of the Forest Service. Standing on hardwood floors, peering through the multi-paned windows above varnished wood cabinets, the structure brings back memories of the 1940s and 50s. It is hard to explain the nostalgia of wooden cabinets to someone younger than 30 years. The reconstruction has remained true to the historic registry while maintaining an illusion of safety by installing a new synthetic wood shingle roof with a Class A fire rating. The multi-pane windows may not keep the cold out but they are historically accurate. The stairs are enclosed with chain link fencing to keep visitors safe.

    If you visit, take a moment to examine the tower's construction. Unlike the slender steel struts of the metal towers, on Buck Mountain massive wooden beams create a solid, heavy structure meant to stand against high winds, lightening strikes and freezing winter temperatures. Archives show the cost of the original structure was less than $1000. The reconstruction costs $55,000. Just another measure of how times have changed since the original tower was built. Buck Mountain is one of the few wooden timber towers remaining throughout the United States, yet it continues to play a vital role in protecting our north land forests. If you want to visit be sure to go during visiting hours. The lookout is closed for two hours at midday.

Buck Mtn.

Coconino National Forest

East Pocket / Coconino National Forest

Tower: East Pocket
Year Built: 1943
Height: 30'
Manufacture: Timber Eng. Corp.
Model: CT-2 wood, 12 x 12 cab

Elevation: 7,198'
District: Peaks / Coconino
Access: Road & Trail
Rating: Active

East Pocket Fire tower has stood watch over Oak Creek Canyon and the Secret Mountain Wilderness since 1943. One of the last of the wood towers, it had fallen into disrepair by the 1980's. When lookout Scott Brownwell first set foot on the tower, his supervisor instructed him to bar visitors from the catwalk for fear the rotten boards would fall away, causing a serious injury. Supervisor Walker Thornton worked hard to allocate limited funds for materials and Scott led the construction effort to restore the catwalk.

During the restoration, The men learned more about how the tower was constructed. Scott realized that the scaffolding for the tower must have gone up first, followed by the catwalk. The cab was constructed on top of the catwalk and forty years later, the boards had turned to mush, disintegrating as he pulled them loose. Today, the tower is a step back into history. As visitors climb the stairs, the massive wood structure seems to close around them, unlike the airy open feel of the steel Aermotor towers built a decade earlier. Along with the catwalk, the windows have been replaced. The original wood shingle roof remains in place.

Scott speculates that the greatest fire danger to the old wooden tower might come from the southwest with the prevailing winds through dense forest. He was less threatened by the fires rising up the steep sides of Oak Creek Canyon, noting that the forest tends to thin out on level ground at the rim. Yet he always knew what escape route he would choose if threatened by fire. In 2003, fire came within 200 yards of the tower.

Due to its remote location, the lookouts at East Pocket see few visitors, about half by trail out of Oak Creek Canyon, the remainder by road. Scott notes that while his primary responsibility is to watch for fires, as an employee of a public agency, he is also available to educate the public about their responsibility to the forest and to answer their questions. Some visitors have never heard of fire towers or their role in protecting the forest. Between standing watch and educating the public, he believes that there is little time for other interests that would distract him from professional responsibilities.

East Pocket

Coconino National Forest

Eldon / Coconino National Forest

Photos taken in 1918 on Mount Eldon show a ground-level wood cabin with a flat roof and a protractor mounted on the roof for spotting fires. In 1913, Forest Service memos advised that a trail should be built from two miles north of Greenlaw's mill to the top of Eldon, a distance of two to three miles, at a cost between $75. and $200. Water was to be delivered twice a week. A telephone was to be installed at a cost of $135.

In those early years, a family lived at the foot of Mt. Eldon, near the mill. It was not uncommon for the mother to call the lookout, asking if he could see her kids in the neighborhood or the surrounding woods. Frequently the lookout would find the kids and send her in the right direction.

In 1953, the cabin was replaced by a fire tower. This tower burned

in the Radio fire in 1977 and was replaced in 1978. The current tower stands watch over the city of Flagstaff and the vast yellow pine forest flowing over the slopes of the San Francisco Peaks.

Sandy, on duty in 2005, started as a relief lookout nine years ago and loves the outdoor feeling conveyed by the windows surrounding her. One of her favorite parts is the adrenalin rush as a fire is spotted and the radio traffic heats up.

As we talked, the phone on the wall rang and Sandy answered, "Eldon Lookout." To some callers, she must explain that she is the lookout. They have no idea what a lookout or fire tower is, and wonder if she is a secretary in an office at the ranger station. With a smile, she recalls those visitors to the tower that start talking the moment they hit the door. They tell her all about fires, firefighting and her job, with no clue, as she says, of the topic they are discussing. We laughed and I made a mental note to make no comment on firefighting, towers and her job for fear that I may be one of the clueless.

As we looked out over the neighboring peaks, she pointed to one slope as the site where hang gliders frequently launch out over the plain below. She said they often call before arriving on site to check the wind velocity. Fifty five mph and above is dangerous. Communication towers crowd the southern edge of the fire tower. She noted that service techs seem to be working on the towers all the time.

A Yorkshire terrier shares the tower with Sandy. A rubber bone lurks near her basket with two tiny dishes for water and food to one side. The Yorkie's ears stand at attention with her tiny pink tongue panting slightly, bright eyes watching every move from a visitor, hoping for a game with the rubber bone.

Before I left the tower, Sandy pointed to a fire close to the Navajo Army Depot. A report comes in that crews are running out of water, the wind is picking up and crew members have been dismissed a bit early. The fire was now beginning to run, spot fires breaking out beyond the fire lines. Instinctively I turned look at Flagstaff and Doney Park, surrounding Mt. Eldon on three sides. As a tower in the urban-forest interface, Eldon lookout carries a tremendous responsibility in lives and property.

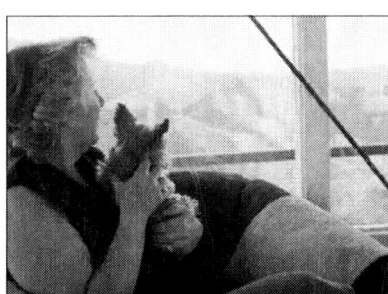

Tower: Eldon	Model:
Year Built: 1977	R-6 flat, 12 x 12 cab
Height: 54'	Elevation: 9,299'
Manufacture: USDA Forest Service	District: Peaks / Coconino
CL 100-106	Access: Road & Trail
	Rating: Active

Eldon

Coconino National Forest

Mount Eldon / The Radio Fire

Mount Eldon stands on the northeast edge of Flagstaff with the Doney Park subdivision spreading along its eastern flanks. The granite slopes are split by a dramatic rocky canyon with accordion rock cliffs and a jumble of boulders and brush littering its floor. In July the summer rains begin to move north out of the Gulf of Mexico and bring relief from the summer heat to the arid southwest. But in June, the air is dry, crackling in the heat. Even though the city sits at 7,000 feet, temperatures may rise to the mid 90's. The brush is tinder dry. The spring grass fades to crisp yellow, all of it susceptible to a tiny spark.

In June 1977, a teenage girl and one, possibly two companions, entered the mouth of the canyon and searched for a campsite along the dry, rocky streambed. They built a campfire, feeding the flames with brush and scraps of branches that littered the sides of the canyon. In the morning, they left, failing to completely extinguish the embers. A dry wind stirred the embers to life, carrying sparks into the dry grass of the canyon.

Dave Patterson was working on the west side of Flagstaff when his son called from their home near the canyon.

"Dad, there's a fire on Eldon. Please come home."

Dave caught the anxious note in his son's voice and raced outside to stare across town at the mountain where a heavy plume of smoke rose above

The Radio Fire, 30 minutes after ignition.

the housetops. He drove quickly over the ridge that separated the east and west side of town to prepare his family for evacuation. Within 30 minutes, the fire had begun to roar up the slopes of Mount Eldon.

The canyon was filled with dry brush and heavy boughed ponderosa pines, their trunks rich in sap. Fire, by nature, always seeks the high ground. The canyon acted as a chute, funneling the heated air from the flames up the side of the mountain. The rising hot air caused the brush and trees to explode into flame as sparks flew upward on the wind currents generated by the heat of the fire.

Word quickly spread across Flagstaff of the fire that had broken out on Eldon and throughout town, people poured into the streets, along sidewalks, watching in awe as the smoke and flames quickly obscured the peak. At times, the smoke parted for a moment and the flames clearly visible, marked the progress of the fire as it roared up the granite slopes. On the peak that towers over the town, the southern end of a long ridge, stands the Eldon fire tower, first built in the early 1900's. Public speculation questioned whether the tower would survive the inferno.

Mount Eldon: The Radio Fire

Mount Eldon engulfed in smoke.

Paul Patterson remembers the smoke parting and catching a glimpse of the tower as it burst into flames. Moments later, the propane tanks near the tower exploded in a fire ball.and then the smoke closed in again. The Pattersons had served as

Coconino National Forest

fire lookouts in Oregon and the Eldon tower was of special interest to them. Watching it burn, after having lived in its shadow, brought a unique

Eldon glowed at night during the Radio Fire.
Photos: Dave Patterson

sense of loss. They understood the promise that the tower held for the resident of Flagstaff in standing watch over the community. Bill and Ellen recall the glowing peak as dusk closed in, pockets of flame spread across the mountainside like Christmas decorations. The residents of East Flagstaff collectively held their breath, hoping for the best. Many hoped the slurry bombers flying over their rooftops would douse the fire before it spread beyond the mountain.

As the flames advanced across Eldon, residents were ordered to evacuate Doney Park due to concern that the fire might descend along the Eldon Ridge into the pinons and junipers that surrounded Koch Field. Not all residents went quietly. Many wanted to stay and fight for their homes. The Forest Service insisted that they leave though some crept back along forest roads to their homes. Val Peavy stood his ground twice, each time being forced to leave. The Daily Sun was to write of his confrontation with a ground crew member over whether the evacuation was mandatory. Fortunately, the flames did not sweep through Doney Park. Two days after it ignited, fire fighters began to gain the upper hand. Five per cent, then fifteen per cent contained. Flagstaff's residents began to hope that their town would escape unscathed.

Twenty eight years later, the scars remain. The exposed granite slopes at the summit are not hospitable ground for new trees to sprout. Brush has moved in but the trees are slow to return. On the grassy peak, the blackened skeletons of ponderosa still line the ridge. For many years, fallen trees formed a maze of giant crisscrossed toothpicks along the upper end of the trail that climbed the peak from east Flagstaff. The city's residents remembered that fire each time they looked up at the peak.

The Eldon tower was rebuilt in 1978 and lookouts continued to stand watch over the cinder hills, the pine forest and the community of Flagstaff. And then it happened again, June 2006. Another call came in from the Eldon Tower, reporting a plume of smoke, rapidly increasing in size on the west side of Flagstaff. A careless motorist had tossed a cigarette out the window of car along West Highway 66. Within five minutes, the smoke had tripled in size. Firefighters sped to the scene to battle the flames as police spread through the neighborhoods along the highway, ordering residents to evacuate. With terror-filled faces, they piled into cars, leaving possessions behind. Some pled for time to find their pets, only to be told that the Red Cross would not permit pets in the shelter.

A day later, firefighters brought the flames under control and residents began to return to their homes. They were angry with the careless motorist, some angry with the police who had worked to save their lives.

June is a bad time for fires in Flagstaff and across the arid southwest. One cigarette or a careless camper can bring a community to a standstill as we wait to see what the flames will take next.

Hutch Mountain / Coconino National Forest

Tower: Hutch Mountain
Year Built: 1936
Height: 31.6'
Manufacture: Aermotor MC-24
Model: L-4, 12 x 12 cab
Elevation: 8,535'
District:
Long Valley / Mogollon Rim / Coconino

Access: Road
Rating: Active

From the Hutch Mountain fire tower, James Nidemeyre maintains watch over Long Lake, Soldier and Tremaine Lakes. With a smile, he says, that the area around the lakes is considered Siberia under his watch. The Forest Service will let a fire burn under control to reduce fire fuels on the ground. He is more concerned about the Blue Ridge community and the residential areas along SR 87 between Winslow and Strawberry. He points out Double Cabin Park is a popular camping area for large groups on three-day weekends. He notes that older people "feel safer in large groups knowing there is a tower nearby as well as the Ranger Station at Happy Jack."

In the late afternoon, visitors can easily see the sun's gleam off the cliffs above Sedona and Oak Creek. James also pointed out a neighboring peak, the site of a massive telescope being built by Lowell Observatory and the University of Arizona, to be completed in five years. It is sponsored by the Discovery Channel who found the remote area ideal for research.

James started working for the Forest Service as a firefighter but like many men he found age catching up with him and began to appreciate the physically less vigorous demands of the lookout. As we talked, I was amazed at the number of people that drove up to the tower. Some turn and leave, others climbed the stairs. On a three-day weekend James may see up to one hundred visitors pass through the cramped cab. Kids are invited to check out the fire finder while adults ask about the notable landmarks. James notes that the tower is showing its age but when asked about maintenance he laughs. Maintenance is not a high priority in a busy district. The previous day the district had over forty fires, many of them from lightening strikes.

Hutch Mountain may have been the site of a 1920's era wooden tower. The current tower was built in 1936 as part of a network of towers that line Forest Highway 3 between State Route 87 and Flagstaff. As I walk down the path from the tower, I meet an older man ascending the short trail climbing toward the tower's base. He announced, with a big smile, "This has been my dream, to climb a lookout tower!" One more visitor to Hutch Mountain.

Hutch Mtn.

Coconino National Forest

Lee Butte / Coconino National Forest

Tower: Lee Butte
Year Built: 1933
Height: 45.9'
Manufacture:
  International Derrick

Model: 7 x 7 cab
Elevation: 7,410'
District: Mormon Lake,
                Coconino
Access: Road
Rating: Inactive

Lee Butte

A narrow dirt road winds through the forest off Forest Highway 3 between Payson and Flagstaff to a lonely fire tower on Lee Butte. Built by the Civilian Conservation Corp in the early 1930's, the tower is only in service under the most dire threat. It stands as part of the chain of towers between Mormon Lake and Long Valley.

Trees crowd the lonely, dark specter. In time, the Forest Service will make a choice whether to cut a few trees down and extend the life of the tower or to decommission the structure. At the base of the tower is a small cabin, originally built as a temporary home for the lookout. A second cabin serves as a storage area. An eerie feeling pervades the site as if there should be something more, maybe the lookout has just stepped out for a moment.

The wind sweeping through the trees is the only constant. At times a truck will pass the tower on the road below the peak, the engine noise abrasive in the deep silence.

The Lee Butte tower resembles those from the Aermotor Company but its manufacturer was International Derrick, one of only five from that manufacturer in Arizona. The cab is seven foot square with a trapdoor in the floor. The Forest Service does rent out some of its cabins and this might be one such property if more interest were expressed in the site.

Buck Mountain, Hutch Mountain and Moqui fire towers now carry the watch for the vast forest that covers the lake country south of Flagstaff.

Coconino National Forest

Mormon Mountain / Coconino National Forest

Mormon Mtn.

The Mormon Lake fire tower tops a little knoll overlooking the area south of the lake, a mere half mile from a busy highway. The access is over a rough dirt track with rocks protruding from a rutted surface to scrape a low undercarriage. It is a favorite area for ATV riders. Many have no idea that the little tower still stands, nearly forgotten. At a gate in the fence on the south side of the dirt track a hikers register marks the trailhead. Most visitors park well below the gate, near FR 124C, and hike the remaining distance along the side road to the tower. One hiker left a comment in the trail head log regarding the beautiful sunset he had watched while sitting at the base of the tower.

The tower was built before the CCC. It's seven foot cab is similar to other towers throughout the region. The small cabin near the tower is literally falling down, one board at a time. Loose boards litter the foundation and floor of the cabin, leaving gaping holes in the wall and ceiling. The cistern, that once provided water for the lookouts, remains uncovered.

A few years ago, the Forest Service tried to give the Mormon Lake fire tower to the Ghost Ranch Museum. When the agreement failed to be completed, the lowest of seven flights of stairs was removed to keep visitors from injury if they should attempt to climb the aging tower.

Forest Service archives note a discussion in favor of giving the tower to the Immigration Service for use on the border with Mexico. The Aermotor tower remains on its lonely knoll with the tree tops slowly encroaching into the view that once held the attention of the lookouts.

Tower: Mormon Lake
Year Built: 1927
Height: 48'
Manufacture: Aermotor LX-24 modified
Model: 7 x7 cab
Elevation: 7,977'
District: Mormon Lake / Coconino
Access: Road
Rating: Inactive

Coconino National Forest

Moqui / Coconino National Forest

Tower: Moqui
Year Built: 1952
Height: 82.6'

Manufacture: USDA Forest Service
CL 100-106
Model: R-6 flat, 14 x 14 cab

Moqui

Moqui fire tower is one of the forest giants, its one hundred foot high steel structure rising out of a clearing above the East Clear Creek Wilderness. East Clear Creek stretches across the southern horizon, a natural break in the undulating carpet of green forest. The most notable man-made feature on the horizon is a massive white Doppler radar dome to the north.

The fire tower is critical for the safety of a rapidly growing area of the state. Small housing developments are springing up across the previously undeveloped area, at risk to wild fire that would devour the dry forests along the rim. When the summer lightening moves in, locals tell the lookout, "keep an eye on my house!"

When this long time lookout first moved from Phoenix to this rural area, she thought she might go crazy living in a tower every day. She took pride in driving the fifty-plus mile stretch of pavement to Winslow in race course time. Now she enjoys slowing down, noting small changes in the forest during leisurely noon-time walks through the thick pines below the tower. She says unlike the competition for the corner office in a corporate world, she's got all four corners in a glass tower with a 360 degree view.

Her tower log records as many as 1,500 visitors in a season, making it one of the busiest towers in the state. Hunters don't hesitate to climb the tower, scouting for deer. If they ask where the animals are, the lookout simply says, "That's why they call it hunting!"

Moqui, a well maintained example of modern tower construction, is very differnt from the austere Aermotor towers of the Depression era. The interior braces in a "K" pattern are further re-inforced by angle braces at each corner. The seven flights rise along the center to a catwalk that surrounds the cab. The fourteen foot square cab is large enough to be a lived in though the current lookout prefers to go home each evening. The modern tower replaced a wooden structure built in 1930. The cabin at the base is no longer used by lookouts.

Elevation: 7,476'
District: Mogollon Rim / Coconino
Access: Road
Rating: Active

Coconino National Forest

O'Leary / Coconino National Forest

Tower: O'Leary
Year Built: 1959
Height: 31.6'
Manufacture: USDA Forest Service CL 100-106
Model: R-6 flat, 12 x 12 cab
Elevation: 8,916'
District: Peaks / Coconino
Access: Road, Visitors must walk road
Rating: Active

O'Leary rises as a steep conical peak out of the Strawberry Crater Wilderness, surrounded by the loose cinder cones of what was once a hot bed of volcanic activity. The lava flows cooled a thousand years ago allowing pines, juniper and wild grasses to cover the surrounding terrain. The Forest Service built the tower in 1959 to stand watch over the eastern side of the San Francisco Peaks as well as the grass parks at the base of Mount Eldon. As Flagstaff has expanded eastward, the O'Leary tower has become incredibly important to the Doney Park region.

Like Volunteer fire tower on the NAD, grassland fires are a major threat to the region east of the peak. In the 1990's a fire swept through the nearby Sunset Crater and Wupatki National Monuments, burning the grass and shrubs. With the vegetation gone, the archeologists discovered many new sites for study.

Standing on an isolated peak, with the trees set back from the tower, O'Leary is a lightening magnet, drawing multiple strikes as the thunderstorms move through each summer. Like most towers, the lookout perches on a chair with glass insulators under each leg when lightening moves over the peak.

In the late 1980's, a wide strip of corrugated metal stretched across a section of hillside below the peak to funnel rainwater into a cistern for the lookout's use. It has since been removed. The tower is live-in for lookouts who choose to stay on the peak.

At one time, it was possible to drive up the peak to the tower. For safety precautions and due to erosion, the Forest Service has closed the road and visitors must hike up to the tower. The lookout actively uses his discretion in allowing visitors to climb the stairs.

O'Leary

Coconino National Forest

Turkey Butte / Coconino National Forest

Tower: Turkey Butte
Year Built: 1937
Height: 31.6'
Manufacture: Aermotor MC-24

Model: L-4, 12 x 12 cab
Elevation: 7,294'
District: Peaks / Coconino
Access: Road
Rating: Active

Turkey Butte

Coconino National Forest

Turkey Butte had been a quiet corner of Arizona, hidden away on a rocky knoll, overlooking the Sycamore Wilderness. Due to the long commute from Flagstaff, the tower had fewer visitors than other towers on the Coconino National Forest. When the Arizona Highways magazine featured the tower in an article, the article wasn't quite clear about its location. Cadillacs and other passenger cars began making the trip from Phoenix, the drivers stuck with the idea that they could make a loop north through Flagstaff, south past Turkey Butte and East Pocket, to drop over the rim to Sedona and back to the valley.

I laughed when I heard about the misunderstanding, noting that it would be a fast and very steep trip down to Sedona, one way! The lookout grimaced and commented that Wilson Mountain might get in the way. For those who don't know the rim country, there is no road from the two towers over the rim to Sedona. The lookout recalled there some very angry drivers who learned they must returned to Flagstaff to make their way south again.

Turkey Butte is a well preserved Aermotor tower with a ten-foot square cab, dating to the CCC era. It replaced the original 20 foot tower which was built in 1916 just ten years after the Forest Service was founded. The cabin at the foot of the knoll has been well maintained and shows the handiwork of a former lookout. When we visited, a double bed occupied one corner with a kitchen counter filling another corner of the room. An overstuffed chair added a bit of comfort along with a wood stove.

Turkey Butte serves as a relay station for crews working in the Sycamore Canyon Wilderness as their signals cannot reach headquarters. The 360 degree view takes in Sycamore Canyon, Apache Maid, Secret Mountain, Mingus Mountain and Prescott. It coordinates calls with Volunteer on the boundary between the Kaibab and the Coconino.

Nearby Ferlow is the site of an old ranger station. Once buzzing with frantic activity during the fire season, it is now rented for a night's stay by application to the Forest Service.

Woody Mountain / Coconino National Forest

Woody Mountain was one of the first two sites on the Coconino to host a fire tower. Before the tower was built, rangers patrolling the forest preserve by horseback used the peak to spot smoke. After the Forest Service was founded in 1905, a small cabin was built at the summit to house a lookout. It was a primitive existence as water was hauled from a nearby spring and supplies packed in by mule.

In 1936, a forty-five foot fire tower manufactured by Pacific Steel replaced the cabin. The tower still stands today, marked by two historic plaques commemorating its history. A small cabin with an attached green house stands at the base of the tower. The outhouse is invaded by ladybugs each year, forming a beaded carpet of red over the fiberglass walls.

When loggers first moved into the area in the early 1900's, they clear cut the forest leaving the peak denuded of all but a few trees. Standing below

Tower: Woody Mountain
Year Built: 1936
Height: 45.9'
Manufacture: Pacific Coast Steel Co.
Rating: Active

Model: 7 x7 cab
Elevation: 8,094'
District: Peaks, Coconino
Access: Road

the tower today, the trees tower overhead, creeping into the view from the small cab. The trees are less than one hundred years old. While we may take it for granted that the trees will simply grow back if clear cut, research has shown that regeneration is very difficult in our arid southwest. Weather, the seed crop and the predation of the elk herds all impede regeneration.

Woody Mountain stands watch over the forest south of Flagstaff, including Rogers Lake. Due to the location, Woody Mountain is frequently visited by campers, some with ill intent. Randall Warner, the lookout, recounted how over July 4, 2006 vandals had ripped the cabin door from its hinges and stolen $500 worth of private possessions and government supplies. He had worked hard to restore the site and was discouraged over the vandalism, including the loss of small solar-powered lights at the base of the tower. He returned by daylight to inspect the damage and insure the vandals were gone, without incurring personal injury. It is irritating that the men and women who stand watch for the public good must suffer at the hands of thieves and vandals.

For those who are interested, former lookout Donna Ashworth has written extensively about the history of Woody Mountain and her own experiences as a lookout on this tower.

Woody Mtn.

Plaques placed at base of tower commemorating the history of the Woody Mountain Fire Tower.

Coconino National Forest

Former Towers / Coconino National Forest

Blue Ridge
Year Built: 1930
Height: 48'
Manufacture: Pacific Coast Steel
Model: 7 x 7 cab
Elevation: 7,416
District: Long Valley

Deadman
Year Built: 1928
Height: 3'
Manufacture: Forest Service
Model: D-6 cupola
Elevation: 7,143'
District: Peaks / Eldon

Mahan Mountain
Year Built: 1916-1917
Height: 30'
Manufacture: Aermotor-LX-24
Model: 7 x 7 cab
Elevation: 8,270'
District: Mogollon Rim

Munds Mountain
Year Built: 1920's
Height: 0'
Manufacture: Forest Service
Model: tree/stand
Elevation: 6,871'
District: Mogollon Rim

Saddle Mountain
Year Built: 1951
Height: 31.6'
Manufacture: Aermotor MC-39
Model: 7 x 7 cab
Elevation: 8,880'
District: Peaks

Slate Mountain
Year Built: 1941
Height: 3'
Manufacture: Forest Service
Model: Wood Cabin
Elevation: 8,215'
District: Peaks

Wing Mountain
Year Built: N/A
Height: 0'
Manufacture: Forest Service
Model: N/A
Elevation: 8,527'

The Navajo Reservation

Chapter 6

Many of the urban residents of Arizona think of the Navajo Reservation as sand and red slick rock based on the terrain they have seen around Page or Monument Valley. The region along the Arizona-New Mexico border is far different from the sparsely-vegetated red sandstone that covers much of the reservation. Green forests with juniper, pinyon, ponderosa, fir and spruce cover dramatic peaks straddling the state line. Much of the landscape along the state line is seldom visited by the white population of the southern region of the state. It is well worth preserving. For those who wish to learn more about the Navajo Reservation, a tour along Route 12 gives an excellent overview of the Navajo Nation.

Five fire towers have been built along the border to stand watch over the forests, guarding a precious resource for the Navajo Nation. Four of these towers have stood for over seventy years, weathering extreme temperatures and deep snow. They are kin to the lookouts who struggle against economic hardship. The fire lookouts of the Navajo Nation do their part to keep fire from blackening the stately forests of their homeland, displaying professional attitudes as they worked under difficult conditions. Only one of the fire towers is located directly off Route 12 but it may possibly be one of the most dramatic in the state as it nestles into a cleft of Black Pinnacle. The other towers require a bit of route finding and are not as accessible.

Navajo Reservation

The Tribe's natural resources are managed jointly by the Bureau of Indian Affairs and Navajo Forestry. While the fire towers are managed by the Bureau of Indian Affairs, the work crews are consolidated under by Navajo Forestry.

The lands of the Navajo Nation cover over 27,000 square miles, the largest Native American reservation in the United States. As a self governing entity, the Nation "seeks to attain economic self-sufficiency while retaining cultural and traditional values". In line with this philosophy, many families maintain small home sites that reflect their culture as they seek employment within the tribal boundaries that will allow self sufficiency. It creates unique challenges for the Tribe, and in turn for Navajo Foestry, as they seek the best of both modern and traditional cultures.

Black Pinnacle / Navajo Reservation

Black Pinnacle is a volcanic remnant that rises above Navajo Route 12 on the Arizona - New Mexico border. The road to the tower wraps around the peak, narrowing to a one lane dirt track. I parked behind the lookout's truck, assured that he wasn't leaving till I left. As I stared up at the little cabin from Route 12, I wondered how the trail would climb the peak's vertical walls. Rounding a rocky bluff, I confronted a flight of steel stairs rising on steel beams to a cleft in the rock. A second flight of stairs nestled between two jutting outcrops as they turned out of sight, into thin air. As I reached the top of the second flight, I found myself at the edge of a sheer drop off, buffeted by the wind. Just a few more steps completed the ascent to the small wood frame cabin. It is as if the cabin had tumbled from the sky, caught on the edge of the cliff, where a stiff gust of window could sweep it to the rocks below. I tried not to look down.

Leon, the lookout on duty, was startled to have a visitor so late in the afternoon. He peered through the door, eyes wide behind thick glasses and allowed me to enter the cabin, leaving the sheer drop off behind. I didn't feel much easier in the wood frame structure though it is wired to the rock. The cabin, similar to an L-4, was built by Navajo Forestry. Where glass windows once gave a 360 degree view, the frames have been reduced to narrow slots of plexiglass - the result of vandalism. The view over the mountains is fantastic as the site straddles the border, dominated by Tsaile Butte.

Leon wishes the job with Navajo Forestry lasted year around as it pays better than the local market. That is the harsh reality of the reservation. Good paying jobs are few. These lookouts maintain a professionalism with an

Black Pinnacle

The first flight of stairs up to Black Pinnacle Fire Tower.

edge of economic reality that they are the fortunate with good paying jobs. Consequently, they sit in tiny bare towers for hours with little action below to relieve the boredom.

As I descended the steel steps, I wondered why Leon, if he liked the money he made working the tower, had never taken the next step toward education and a full time job in forestry. So I stopped him ten minutes later as he barreled down the road in an old pick up truck and asked him that question. He looked blank for a moment and then quietly said, "I never thought of it." Again the reality of the Reservation. So many young people fail to catch the vision of higher education and the opportunity it presents for the future. I hope he pursues the opportunity.

Tower: Black Pinnacle	Model: Wood Cabin
Year Built: 1936	Elevation: 7,938'
Height: 3'	Access: Trail
Manufacture: Navajo Tribe	Rating: Active

Navajo Reservation

Fluted Rock / Navajo Reservation

Fluted Rock is a black volcanic extrusion set among green rolling hills and meadows, dotted by ponderosa pine. To reach the tower, visitors climb out of thick stands of Mexican locust to a small saddle with a blackened, moonscape appearance that seems out of place as it rises out of the green forests. The tower is not visible from the saddle. The route across the moonscape is outlined by volcanic rock to give some clue as to the location of the tower. Considering the setting, it is one of the most unusual geologic formations I have climbed in Arizona and without doubt one of the most beautiful.

I found the gate in the fence around the forty foot tower locked and called repeatedly before the lookout responded. I learned that two intoxi-

cated individuals had left her very anxious and she had locked the gate for her own safety. She was the relief for the regular lookout on his day off. In thinking about the isolation for a woman alone in the tower, I didn't envy her position.

After visiting Oak Ridge and Piney Hill, this tower seems a bit stunted by comparison. All three date to the 1930's but there seems to be no record about who raised the towers. Two cement slabs mark the site where an A-frame cabin sat on the volcanic peak until rats left the structure unsafe for human use. It was replaced by the Aermotor tower.

Recent visitors, or possibly the lookouts, have left their mark by arranging loose rock to spell their names on the flat hilltop. The names are easily recognizable when viewed from the cab of the tower.

The landscape, stretching out from the base of the hill, is an artist's dream of meadows and small water tanks among groves of trees. The meadows surrounding Fluted Rock are popular for sheep grazing and several sheep camps are visible from the tower. It would be a tragedy if fire blackened the region. Before calling in a fire, the lookouts are careful to check with headquarters on whether a smoke column rises from a burning trash pile or if it is cause for alarm.

As I walked back down the road, I heard a cow bell in the forest below. I thought about the two individuals who had threatened the lookout earlier and realized that I shared her concerns in my own isolation. I walked a little faster, casting a quick glance over my shoulder.

Fluted Rock

Navajo Reservation

Tower: Fluted Rock
Year Built: 1930's
Height: 41.3'
Manufacture: Aermotor MC-39
Model: 7 x 7 cab
Elevation: 8304'
Access: Road
Rating: Active

Oak Ridge / Navajo Reservation

Driving along Oak Ridge from the dispatch center at Windowrock, I began to wonder where the tower was located as the miles added up and I failed to see a tower on the horizon. And then along the light brown dirt road, the signed turnoff appeared and the tower suddenly made an appearance above the trees. The original tower, a wood structure, was first located about three miles south of its current location. It was moved due to private land allotments and safety concerns.

I pulled into the parking area below the tower and stepped from the car to gaze up into an enormous pair of binoculars plastered to the face of the lookout as he leaned out of the window staring down at me. I waved and began climbing the ten flights of stairs.

Ricky, the lookout, is a wiry middle-aged man fueled by nervous

Tower: Oak Ridge
Year Built: 1941
Height: 82.6'
Manufacture:
   International Derrick
Model: 7 x 7 cab
Elevation: 7528'
Access: Road
Rating: Active

energy. As I described my interest in the fire towers, he began to point out the few landmarks on the horizon and I realized what had seemed out of place about this location. It was flat! A sea of trees, seeming to be all the same height stretched in every direction. A distant range of low hills broke the horizon. The tower is the only high point for observation. Local residents stop by to ask if Ricky has seen a favorite horse, a cow or a herd of sheep that have wandered beyond expectation.

I recalled a conversation with a Navajo Forestry fire tech. He had complained that the forest was not healthy. Looking at the crowded trees all at the same height, I gained an appreciation for his concern as I thought of a fire sweeping along the ridge.

Along with watching for smoke, Ricky makes meticulous observations on temperature, precipitation and wind speed. Pulling out a plastic case, he leaned out the window.

Oak Ridge

Uncapping a tube in the center of the case, he extended his arm out the window and placed a finger over the end of the tube. He noted the displacement on the device and told me the winds were topping out at twenty-five miles per hour. We listened to the wind slipping around the tower and I thought about descending the ten flights of stairs holding tightly to the railing as the wind gusts sweep through the metal scaffolding.

Navajo Reservation

109

Piney Hill / Navajo Reservation

Piney Hill

Piney Hill is one of a string of fire towers along the Arizona-New Mexico border on the Navajo Reservation. The Aermotor tower was built in the 1930's and is showing the effects of decades of wind, snow and rain. The windows have been replaced but the tower needs more maintenance. Like Oak Ridge, the Piney Hill tower stands on a plateau, the highest point for observation of smoke or lost livestock.

After driving up to the tower, some visitors gaze up at the eighty foot tower and choose not to climb the twelve flights of stairs. For Teresa, a young Navajo woman on duty, the tower may be something of a refuge from the everyday demands of eight children. When I asked her if she took the job for a little peace and quiet, she simply smiled in response. Previously she had worked for a local boarding school and the quiet of the tower just may be something she sought after years of supervising young children.

From her tower she can see the dramatic ridge that rises above the Navajo capitol of Windowrock with the red cliffs gleaming in the sun. The area around the Windowrock is juniper and pinyon country. The tower sits at a higher elevation in ponderosa pine. It is a quiet refuge from the hustle of the town, set in a meadow of wild grass with pines well-spaced in a forest that appears to have been previously thinned to quell the fire danger.

During the winter Teresa spends the time at home with her family. She told me her husband works for tribal forestry. His job involves home inspections, wood cutting, fires/fire investigation and patrolling the forest. It would seem their jobs neatly dovetail, each supporting the other.

Tower: Piney Hill
Year Built: 1930's
Height: 81'
Manufacture: Aermotor MC-39
Model: 7 x 7 cab
Elevation: 8102'
Access: Road
Rating: Active

Navajo Reservation

Roof Butte / Navajo Reservation

Taking the road to Roof Butte, I entered one of the most beautiful areas on the reservation. The route follows Tsaile Creek, a sparkling stream between grassy banks with tall spruce and fir climbing the ridge on either side. At one point, I took the wrong fork and reached a high plain with little sheep camps in every direction. Curious cows eyed the car crowding their space along the narrow road. It all came with a sense of isolation. I retraced my route and moved on, stopping for a moment to stretch my legs. Then came the sound of an engine, climbing the hill below me. I had not passed a single vehicle along

Tower: Roof Butte
Year Built: 1960
Height: 15'
Manufacture: Navajo Tribe
Model:
   7 x 7 cab on expanded metal platform
Elevation: 9783'
Access: Road
Rating: Active

Roof Butte

Navajo Reservation

the road. As I returned to the car, a communications truck swept past me. I quickly followed him. In time he pulled over and asked if I was lost, possibly on my way to Shiprock? When I told him I was headed to same place he was, he looked astonished and asked if I meant the towers. I assured him I did and would be following in his tracks the remaining two miles. I noticed that after each rough spot he would slow, watching my vehicle. As we topped out on Roof Butte, I failed to see the tower. With a bit of chagrin, I asked where the tower was and he replied, with a smile, that I was not looking. I once again looked around and found an unassuming structure in the shadow of the giant communication towers, a one story metal platform with a glass cabin set in the middle of the metal grating.

Ken, the lookout, stepped out of a small two room cabin and introduced me to his corner of Arizona. On one side of the ridge, the desert highlands north of Canyon de Chelly are a mosaic of sun and shadow stretching out to Monument Valley on a clear day. On the opposite side, one would think of Colorado with fir and spruce sweeping over jagged peaks. Ken says that if he tires of one view, he simply turns and looks at an entirely different landscape.

Ken arrives early in the season, sometimes using his truck to barrel through snow drifts covering the road. The fire tower was built in 1960 by Navajo Forestry and it is unique among the state's towers. Built of metal and glass, no wood, it would seem to be a magnet for lightening strikes. Though the fire tower is crowded up against communications towers, Ken rejects the idea of moving to a neighboring ridge. He appreciates the visitors the towers bring to his lookout.

When he was younger, Ken chose to fight fires. "When you're young, you'll try anything," he says. "Then I got older and wised up. Now I spot smoke for those guys." He recalled a big fire near Carrizo in 2004. He watched the flames comes over the mountain under a huge column of smoke, hots spots breaking out ahead of the fire.

He likes being his own boss and likes having the winters off. He expects to do the job a couple more years and then move on to another calling.

A Profile from Native Lands

Much of the land in the northeastern corner of Arizona and the White Mountains is allotted to Native American tribes. It is governed by Tribal Councils, who work in cooperation with the Bureau of Indian Affairs. The relationship between the Native tribes and the federal government has often been a rocky one, with the Federal government's intent repeatedly switching between self governance and treating the tribes as wards. This is reflected in the Forestry programs on each of the Reservations. Currently the trend is toward self governance with the tribes taking responsibility for much of what occurs on their lands.

The Forestry programs for the tribes first began receiving funding in the 1940's. The programs were not always adequately funded. When Reservation lands came under the National Wildfire Danger Rating System, financial backing for the forestry programs increased. Yet, like many federal programs, it can be argued that there are never adequate financial resources to accomplish all the goals set forth. Adding to the angst of financial shortfalls, decisions about the land and how resources are used are often made in a central office away from the reservations. The technicians with experience on the ground have limited input into the decisions that affect their forests.

On both the Navajo and Fort Apache Reservation I heard concern expressed about the health of the forest and the decisions being made in offices outside the reservations. On the White Mountain Reservation it was explained to me that the tribal council often made decisions about grazing that were based not on the knowledge of sound forestry but rather tribal politics. A former BIA supervisor expressed his concern that the native lands on both the Hualapai and San Carlos Reservations had been heavily overgrazed with the tribes now paying the price in the deterioration of the forest. Fire techs on three reservations pointed to crowded trees and single story forest canopies as examples of poor forest health.

Four of the larger reservations with forested lands have fire towers to stand watch over their timber. The lookouts are seasonal employees of the BIA yet work closely with the crews on the ground managed by tribal forestry. Despite the challenges, the tribal employees are proud of the work they do and try to maintain a professional standard.

Jonah Bizardi has worked in many aspects of forestry on the Navajo Reservation for as long as any of his fellow employees can remember. Jonah is not telling just how many years that has been but he does recall the early days when things were done much differently than now.

As a teenager, he had begun to get into trouble. His mother knew the fire control ranger. She talked to the ranger about putting Jonah to work to keep him out of trouble. The ranger told him to bring three weeks worth of food and supplies. This was sufficient warning that he was headed for a very remote area. The ranger took him to Roof Butte and dropped him off. There he stayed for three weeks at a time. He recalls the fire cabin at Roof Butte as an A frame shack with three windows, one each looking east, south and west. He says it was like sitting on a dome, on top of the world.

I mentioned that Bill Watchman, the dispatch coordinator, called Roof Butte the Shangri-La of the reservation.

"Before the communication towers went up," Jonah sneered.

As I drove up to Roof Butte, I began to understand his disapproval. The current tower is dwarfed by giant steel towers, crowding the little cab. The views are spectacular, the top of the peak is not! Jonah has suggested moving the fire tower to a neighboring peak. The current lookout wants the tower to stay where it is with the communication towers around him.

Jonah recalled that water and gas were trucked in for the men stationed at Roof Butte. Supply crews drove to within a quarter mile of the peak where the real work began as they carted fifty-five gallon drums of fuel up the rocky trail. Gas-powered generators recharged the batteries for their military radios. Jonah credits this early experience with learning to cook and for his expertise in chopping wood. Their only source of heat was a wood stove for cooking and keeping warm on cold evenings.

In the 1950's, two-man teams worked the fire towers and cabins. One was a lookout, the other chased down the plumes of smoke and extinguished the fires. If a smoke chaser needed help with the fire, he would go down to the nearest trading post and hire three or four men to work as a fire crew until the fire was extinguished. In the 1950's this may have been one of the few sources of income originating outside the reservation.

In relating the history of the lookouts, Jonah interrupted his memories of Roof Butte in the 1950's to recite the radio frequencies as called in by the lookouts. KOJ586 was

Roof Butte where he was first assigned. KOJ583 was at Tohatchi, east of Navajo. A forty-foot tower sent the signal for KOJ584 at Black Pinnacle. He stopped to tell me that this was originally the base for a range rider in the saddle each day. The rider's base was an L-4 cabin at the foot of the peak. Jonah talked about Tohri, east of the escarpment at Chuska in New Mexico, one of the two tallest towers on the Navajo Reservation. The site was originally south of Two Grey Hills, based in a shack facing west. His comment reminded me of the Two Grey Hills pattern so famous in Navajo weaving. But Jonah moved on to KOJ582 at Oak Ridge. He remembers the original wood tower, located three or four miles south of its current location. Then he called out KOJ581 at Piney Hill, followed by KOJ580 at Fluted Rock. Originally an A-frame cabin sat on the volcanic peak until rats left the structure unsafe for human use. The old cabin is gone, replaced by a forty-foot tower.

Returning to his account of the towers, he recalled that in 1959 the Forestry Department began construction for a new tower at Roof Butte by building a road to the site. This would eventually allow the communications towers to intrude on the peak as well. Navajo Forestry discontinued the use of two men teams at each site in 1965 due to lack of funding. Under the National Wildfire Danger Rating system, fire crews were established throughout the nation and this provided employment opportunities for more people on the Reservation. Jonah still believes that the two-men teams were a better system. He decries the lack of interest in personal responsibility and self improvement today. He recalled studying trigonometry in the tower as he stood watch. In the old days, lookouts worked for pin point accuracy. Comfort was not a factor. Duty was important.

Jonah spoke with pride of his schedule for the last fifteen years. He arrives at the office by 7:00 a.m. for morning prayers and works till 6:30 in the evening. He does not officially clock in till 8:00, it is the sense of duty that dictates the hours.

Forestry is a source of income for the Tribes, either through timber sales, or cutting poles and firewood. For the Navajos, their priorities are in timber sales, fire prevention and forest development. Forest development includes fire management, monitoring disease including ravages of the bark beetle, inventory and timber stand improvement.

Jonah believes that the department does not manage the forest consistently. He is concerned that they do not clean up the terrain after a timber sale. He believes that the tribe fails to see the value of their forests and how the lack of logging is hurting the tribe as well as the forests. He thinks the current practices in logging encourage even-age forest rather the multi-story forests that are healthier for the trees, people and animals. He cites areas near Fluted Rock, Tohatchi and Black Pinnacle as old growth forests and believes selective logging as opposed to clear cutting improves the forest.

As we talked, Jonah surprised me by stating that the Navajos need to learn how to use their land for the benefit of all. He pointed to the White Mountain Apaches as an example of a tribe that is community oriented, working together to make the most of the value of their land. He pointed back to the earliest days when bands of Apaches hunted as units, living in small communities. He talked about looking for the beauty of the creation, setting aside special areas for the good of all rather than using every area for home sites. As we talked about the Apaches, my thoughts turned to the ski resort at Sunrise and the recreational opportunities on the White Mountain Apache Reservation. The Apache Tribe has benefitted from their recreational enterprise for years. I recalled the small communities at White River and McNary on the Fort Apache Reservation with tribal members living in traditional neighborhoods. By contrast, on Roof Butte, I recalled Jonah's statements as I drove through a highland dotted by small summer camps. I've been told that each family is allotted a home site by the tribe but may also claim a site for a sheep camp during the summer.

I looked at Tsaile Creek and thought about the economic possibilities for a campground, catering to white visitors. As I showed the photos of Tsaile Creek with its lush spruce and fir forests, green meadows and sparkling stream to a friend, he declared that this could be on the Navajo Reservation. And I understood Jonah's point. The Navajos are missing out on an economic opportunity for the sake of their tradition.

Months later, I mentioned these ideas to Bob McNichols, a former BIA Supervisor on the Hualapai range. He noted that for many years on the Hualapai Reservation the timber industry took second seat to grazing as the tribe expanded their irrigation capacity with over 300 miles of pipeline. A large percentage of tribal members live in Peach Springs, their tribal headquarters along US66. Yet Bob now considers the Reservation to have been harmed by overgrazing without the community showing long term benefits. Land management is a complicated issue.

The consideration of forest management on tribal lands is a microcosm for what ails the larger global community with its conflict between development and the public good. For the Tribes however, the argument pushes very close to their economic survival as there are so few opportunities on Arizona's Reservations. Those opportunities have not always been used wisely and Tribal economies have suffered. Add in the conflict between big government represented by the Bureau of Indian Affairs and the desire for local management by the Tribal council and the picture becomes even more complicated. As a result, the forests pay the price in being poorly managed.

As I listened to the last few comments from Jonah, I studied the flat planes of his facial features that evoke strong memories of some of the historic photos of his ancestors. He is a bridge between two generations. He represents discipline and personal transformation, mourning the past while looking into the future. He is a fire tech. It is his job to leave a heritage, represented by the forest, to be managed by the next generation.

Apache-Sitgreaves Nat'l. Forest
Chapter 7

The Apache - Sigreaves National Forest covers over two million acres in eastern Arizona with the elevation ranging from 3,000 feet near Clifton to around 11,000 feet at the peak of Mount Baldy. Between these two extremes, the terrain varies from desert grassland to juniper pinon into ponderosa pine and fir trees. The two forests were combined in 1974 under a central administration in the Supervisors office in Springerville.

The Apache Forest spreads along the border with New Mexico, encompassing Mount Baldy, the Escudilla and Bear Wallow Wilderness areas as well as the Blue Range Primitive area. The Sitgreaves Forest spreads eastward from its border with the Coconino south of Flagstaff, along the Mogollon Rim to the border with the Apache just west of Springerville. It encompasses a number of small communities that are at high risk of wildfire. The urban interface between these communities and the forest has become a hot topic for those who support thinning the forests to protect homes and lives against wild fire.

Together the two forests have thirty-four lakes and reservoirs along with over 680 miles of rivers and streams. The region receives the most precipitation of any throughout Arizona, leaving it a special delight for water hungry Arizonans. However, all the moisture also means lush forests with heavy undergrowth. When a fire starts in the Apache Sitgreaves, it has a lot of fuel to feed the flames.

The Apache National Forest includes districts Alpine, Clifton, and Springerville while the Sitgreaves includes districts Black Mesa, Payson, Chevelon, Heber and Lakeside. The Apache NF has eight fire towers while the Sitgreaves has seven. Six other sites have been documented as locations from which towers that have been removed. Tower sites range from primitive isolation to urban interface, creating a great diversity for the lookouts that watch the forest.

The management concerns of the Apache-Sitgreaves focus on the health and restoration of watersheds, sustaining forest ecosystems, reducing danger from wildfire in the urban interface and maintaining their road system. Improving customer service has also been made a priority in a region that depends heavily on tourism for economic sustenance.

Apache Sitgreaves National Forest

Bear Mountain / Apache Sitgreaves Natl. Forest

Photo: A-S National Forest Archives.

Tower: Bear Mountain
Year Built: 1933
Height: 45.9
Manufacture:
    Aermotor LX-25

Model: 7x7 cab
Elevation: 8,550'
District:
    Alpine / Apache Sitgreaves
Access: Trail
Rating: Inactive

Bear Mountain

Apache Sitgreaves National Forest

Bear Mountain Fire Tower has the longest commute in Arizona for a fire lookout. No road leads to the tower that sits just five and a half miles west of the New Mexico border in the Blue Range Wilderness area. Lookouts must hike seven and a half miles to the tower. Manufactured by Aermotor, as LX-25, the tower has a seven foot square cab. It is the only tower in Arizona to have a ladder that runs up the outside of the forty-five foot structure to the cab.

Two small cabins and a corral stand near the tower, one of them used as living quarters, the other as a cache for fire crews. When the tower was actively manned, the Forest Service assigned a family to the site. In their younger years, the kids were packed in along with supplies by pack horse to spend their summers on the tower. One summer they were forced to evacuate the site as a wildfire swept through the Blue Range. With a seven mile commute by foot, the lookout required a full day for evacuation. They didn't take any chances.

Over seven decades, the trees have grown up around the 1930's era tower, crowding the panorama. The tower is part of a chain of lookouts that included the Blue and Rose Peak to the west and the Escudilla to the north. Between the four towers, the lookouts covered much of the Blue Range and the watershed of the Blue River. A true sense of comaraderie developed, flowing over the radio waves between the isolated lookouts.

Bear Mountain has remained the most difficult to reach, the only tower between the Blue River and the New Mexico border. Even with modern equipment, the Blue Range continues to be one of the most remote areas in Arizona. When fires break out in the Blue Range they are expensive to fight due to the rugged terrain and limited access. It is often easier to monitor the fire's progress rather than stage an aggressive campaign to suppress the fire.

Today Bear Mountain is no longer in active service due to the long hike in to the tower, the cost of maintenance and the use of aerial reconnaissance. Rose Peak and Escudilla are the only two towers covering the vast area along the Arizona - New Mexico border. Towers in New Mexico may provide a cross check for any sightings.

Big Lake / Apache Sitgreaves National Forest

Standing in the cab of the Big Lake Fire Tower, a panorama of lakes and forest-covered peaks, streams and dirt roads stretch out before the observer. Above the windows of the cab, a lookout has neatly inked the names of the landmarks spread across the horizon along with distance and degrees. With a

Tower: Big Lake
Year Built: 1967
Height: 31.6
Manufacture: Aermotor MC-24
Model: L-4, 7x7 cab

Elevation: 9,415'
District: Alpine / Apache-Sitgreaves
Acess: Road & Trail
Rating: Active

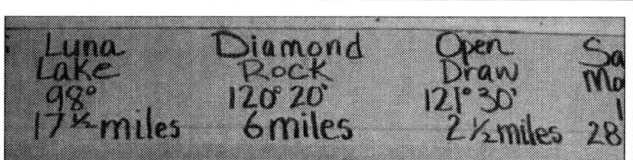

smile, the lookout at Reno Tower suggests that maybe the lookouts at Big Lake have too much time on their hands. The gentle humor is common among the lookouts, all proud of the work they do in protecting the forest. However perceived, I liked looking at the names and identifying each landmark as we surveyed the horizon.

On the day we visited, the tower had closed for the season but a maintenance person worked inside, bringing the ceiling of the cab back into good condition. His hammer strokes echoed through the forest. Maintenance to the towers may be one of the lower priorities on a National Forest, depending on the amount of revenue generated and other demands within the district. As I visited each tower, I found a wide range of conditions. Some towers sprouted peeling paint, single pane windows and rickety wood floors with steps that creaked under mounting pressure. Others showed extra care from their lookouts. Most had been modified from the original design but still manage to hang onto the National Historic Register designation. They stand as a marker in time of construction technique and what is deemed acceptable for human habitation within a given culture. While the priority of surveillance remains important, the historic designation has left many towers as relics to standards of an earlier era.

The Big Lake Tower stands at the edge of a rocky cliff on a little knob southeast of Big Lake. A long set of stairs climbs to the base of the tower from the parking area. A cabin at the base of the stairs, no longer inhabited, once offered shelter to the lookout and his horse. Aspen and fir crowd the base and threaten the view as time passes. Few visitors choose to follow the footpath from the peak's base or drive the access road to the tower. That seems odd as it remains one of the most accessible towers in the state for those visiting the White Mountains.

Big Lake

Apache Sitgreaves National Forest

123

Blue / Apache Sitgreaves National Forest

Photo:
A-S
National
Forest
Archives

Tower: Blue
Year Built: 1933
Height: 31.6
Manufacture: Aermotor MC-24
Model: 10 x 10 cab
Elevation: 9,346'
District: Alpine / Apache-Sitgreaves
Access: Trail
Rating: Inactive, under consideration for Decommission

Blackened trees stand as mute witness to the role of a fire lookout along the trail to the Blue Fire Tower. The undergrowth has begun to recover but it will be years before new trees replace the blackened sentinels. As I walked along the trail, the dead trees creaked, a warning to hikers of how unsafe the site of an old fire can be, a promise that these trees will fall and rot to nourish the soil for new seedlings.

The Blue Fire Tower is only accessible by trail from a trail head six miles east of US191. It stands in an official wilderness area. The Forest Service has condemned the tower. Pack rats and deer mice have invaded the cab, shredding the mattress, leaving urine and feces behind that may contain the threat of hantavirus. The tower is in poor condition, the steps and floor rotting. It is not a safe place to go. An old cistern near the tower, its cover missing, reminds visitors of the basic requirements of the lookouts that stood watch. Yet there is something mystical about the lone structure silhouetted against the sky on a minor peak overlooking the drainage of the Blue River.

Is the Blue Tower still needed? Tower buffs would insist that it can still serve a purpose. Charlotte Hunter, the Forest Archeologist, explained that as the district budget moves down the chain of command from Washington to the National Forest, each office takes a slice of the funds directed to the Forest. The remaining amount leaves little for archeological research, restoration and record keeping. Fire towers are not a high priority though she wishes there were more resources for all the historical sites on the Forest. As we discussed the process to first decommission and then abandon the tower, she received a call for information on the Blue tower. After the call, she told me she suspects the caller is preparing for the fight to keep the tower in service even though it may not be actively used. She made the statement impassively, already having described the shortage of funds for the district and her position. She could use the time and effort for something more productive. I wondered if the tower could be restored or moved to another location. Charlotte seemed open to the idea. The truth is that her days are full and she does not have the time to pursue every good idea.

Blue

Apache Sitgreaves National Forest

Deer Springs / Apache Sitgreaves Natl. Forest

Tower: Deer Springs
Year Built: 1923
Height: 50'
Manufacture: Aermotor LL-25
Model: 7x7 wood cab
Elevation: 7,256'
District: Black Mesa / Apache-Sitgreaves
Access: Road
Rating: Active

Deer Springs Fire Tower stands watch on FR300, a popular route along the Mogollon Rim. The site has the distinction of bright yellow letters that spell out "Deer Springs" on the roof of the cabin at the base of the tower. There is no record of who first painted the sign but Forest personnel assume that it was done as a landmark for low flying aircraft. Having flown out to some of the towers in eastern Arizona, I can appreciate the help in identifying a particular tower from the air.

The tower was not used for several years after the Chediski fire burned through the area in 2002. In 2006, the Forest Service fire management officer was considering assigning a lookout to the tower as the grass and shrubs had revegetated under what remained of the forest canopy. Without adequate snowfall during the winter of 2005, the brush was very dry, standing upright, untouched by heavy snow.

Although the tower had not been staffed since 2002, the Forest Service sent out engine crews every couple of weeks to check the site and monitor the surrounding area for a few hours. The site on the Mogollon Rim is a valuable location as the escarpment rises nearly two thousand feet over the region below, offering the fire crews an expansive view over the forest.

The ridge top around the tower is cobblestone and gravel. In 2002, as the Chediski fire began to move northward across the Fort Apache Reservation, the Black Mesa district personnel knew the flames were coming toward the tower. They worked quickly to clean up the area, reducing the fuel for the fire. A sixty-five foot diameter was cleared of brush and small diameter timber. The bare ground around the tower is evidence of their effort to protect the structure. The fire burned in a mosaic pattern across the ridge and around the tower, but the tower and cabin still stand without damage.

The tower is frequently visited by those who drive the scenic route along the rim. Some of the visitors are surprised to enter the clearing and find the tower. It can be an educational experience as they learn more about the role of the Forest Service in protecting our forests.

Deer Springs

Apache Sitgreaves National Forest

Escudilla / Apache Sigreaves National Forest

Tower: Escudilla
Year Built: 1965
Height: 54'
Manufacture: USDA Forest Service CL 100-106
Model: R-6 flat, 12 x 12 steel cab
Elevation: 10,876'
District: Alpine / Apache-Sitgreaves
Access: Trail
Rating: Active

Escudilla

Apache Sitgreaves National Forest

Escudilla Fire Tower is located north of the little town of Alpine on the New Mexico border. The tower, stands on a rocky bluff, overlooking the heavy, deep green spruce and fir forests that line Alpine Pass along US191 and the meadows of the Williamson Valley. There is no road to the summit on Excudilla Peak. Lookouts hike two and half miles from a parking area halfway up the mountain to their work assignment. All supplies and equipment must be carried in.

In 2005, the lookout at Reno Fire Tower, had just moved over from Escudilla. For years he would reach the trail head by 6:30 in the morning, hiking through the chill dawn to report on duty by 8:00. He would return to the trail head after dark and drive home, only to rise early the next morning to start over once again. The extended schedule made for very long days though he could have chosen to live in the tower, returning home on days off. After years of serving at Escudilla, he grew tired of the wind and cold that haunts this exposed location. He grew tired of the short evenings at home and chose to stand watch in a more hospitable location.

The trail to Escudilla is tough, beginning with a steep ascent through an aspen forest. It mellows out a bit across a wide stretch of alpine meadow before a final steep ascent to the tower. From the catwalk surrounding the tower, the lookout often heard the voices of visitors coming up the trail. When they failed to make an appearance, he believed they turned back just short of the tower, deterred by the final, steep ascent.

Despite the distance and the steep climb, the tower is visited by over 800 people each summer. The view is worth the effort expended to reach the tower as an awesome panorama spreads below the peak. Dark purple mountain ranges march into New Mexico and south toward Clifton-Morenci. Deep green forests cover the mountains, contrasting with the pale yellow of the dry plains near Springerville spread out below the peak. As visitors catch their breath, they are a bit awed by the landscape that the lookout surveys daily in his turn at watch. Built in 1965, the forty year old tower is one of the newest of the state towers. It is identical to Reno, its sister tower located south of Alpine

Gentry / Apache Sitgreaves National Forest

Tower: Gentry
Year Built: 1965
Height: 67'
Manufacture:
  USDA Forest Service
  CL100-106

Model: R-6 flat, 12 x 12 cab
Elevation: 7,724'
District: Black Mesa /
  Apache Sitgreaves
Access: Road
Rating: Active

The term 'urban interface' defines the tight margin for small communities that live on the fringe of the forest, facing the threat of wild fire. The communities along Route 260, Heber, Overgaard and Clay Springs, are an excellent example of the danger represented by urban interface. In June 2002, that threat became very real as flames ignited near the Chediski tower on the Apache Reservation.

As the Rodeo-Chediski Fire began its run through the Reservation forest, the district knew it was headed in the direction of Gentry and Deer Springs towers as well as the communities along Route 260. Crews moved in to clean up the area around the towers in the fire's path, leaving limited ground cover to burn. To reduce the amount of fuel for a fire, the crews cut the thickets of crowded little pines along with dense brush and stacked the remains in slash piles. In an average year, these slash piles would be burned in early spring to clear out potential fire tinder. On average, crews will clean out a sixty-five foot diameter around a building. As the Chediski fire approached, this margin was increased to a hundred twenty feet out from the Gentry tower, improving its fire protection zone.

After clearing the brush, the crews soaked the tower with water and then left. They waited to hear whether the structure would survive the onslaught of the flames. When we visited the tower, the trees seemed to close in around the tower and I was amazed that the flames had not damaged the structure. The trees stand as witness to the tremendous effort of the crews to stop the flames.

The tower, built in 1965, is a more recent addition to the historic structures that have stood seventy years. Unlike the Aermotor towers of an earlier era, the structure takes on a solid appearance with stair and platforms solidly balanced along the ascent. The cab, surrounded by a catwalk, could be a live-in arrangement if the lookout chose to stay at night.

Due to its location on FR300, the lookout sees fewer visitors than towers further west on this popular route. After the Rodeo-Chediski Fire, the number of visitors picked up briefly as people came out to see the damage from the massive fire, spread across 500,000 acres of once forested land.

Gentry

Apache Sitgreaves National Forest

Greens Peak / Apache Sitgreaves Natl. Forest

Tower: Greens Peak
Year Built: 1962
Height: 54'
Manufacture: USDA Forest Service CL100-106
Model: R-6 flat, 12 x 12 cab
Elevation: 10,115'
District: Springerville / Apache Sitgreaves
Access: Road
Rating: Active

Greens Peak

Apache Sitgreaves National Forest

Approaching Greens Peak, the road cuts diagonally across the face of a steep slope devoid of trees. It is a dramatic approach to the 1960's era fire tower. The southeastern side of the peak is covered with wild grass and was once considered as a site for a ski run. The surface of the road undulates across the side of the peak, a sharp drop off without guard rails to one side. The north side of the peak is heavily forested. The views from the top are spectacular, a landscape of forest covered peaks, meadows and small lakes. All of it leaving visitors with the wish to simply spend a long time, soaking up the quiet of Greens Peak.

The fire tower is a modern, solid structure with a live-in cab set apart from the communication tower site. The tower is used by several agencies as a platform for both UHF and VHF antennas. The National Weather Service maintains an antenna on the roof while both Customs and the Forest Service have their own networks. Even Animal Control has a receptor to aid their communication.

We found radio tech Clarence "Mack" MacMillian working on the tower. He says he has the best job in the Forest Service keeping personnel on the air over three National Forests. He loves getting out of the office, into the beautiful mountain ranges of Arizona. Before he came to Arizona, he worked in both Alaska and the Carson National Forest in New Mexico. Our arid state is a far cry from the demands of Alaskan terrain where all towers were either serviced by air or boat. But the high peaks of Arizona still present a bit of a challenge during the winter when Mack fires up the snow cat, the tracks churning up snow-covered slopes with temperatures and wind chill sometimes well below zero.

It is a job one has to love to endure the harsh conditions, ranging from sub zero temperatures to sweltering summer afternoons, driving long miles over four-wheel drive roads between each tower. As if conditions weren't tough enough, due to budget cuts, the number of technicians employed by the Forest Service nationwide has dropped from 1400 to 638, leaving more work for those who remain. It is a job the technicians have to love if they are to remain more than a couple of years working with a public agency.

133

Juniper Ridge / Apache Sitgreaves Natl. Forest

Juniper Ridge

Juniper Ridge fire tower stands watch over the western edge of Showlow and all the little communities along State Route 260. The tower's role came to the forefront as the Rodeo and Chediski fires began to devour the forest south of the highway. Along with the fires crews, the lookout monitored the fire's progress until being evacuated from the fire's path. The ridge supporting the tower did not fare so well. Driving up to the tower, grass has begun to cover the scars of the fire but it will be years before the trees begin to stake their claim on the loose soil. Erosion has begun to cut gullies down the steep slopes. Fallen tree stumps litter the hill reminding visitors of the fire that once swept over the ridge. The tower remains but the fire destroyed the forest surrounding it. Juniper Ridge was one of the casualties of the fire.

The fifty foot plus tower was built in 1959 by the Forest Service. In the 1970's, the tower was renovated. Maintenance crews failed to understand the strict requirements of the historical register. They moved into Juniper Ridge to update the interior and make other changes. The Historical Register requires that a structure listed in their data base remain unchanged from its original premise. If maintenance is required, the same materials must be used, along with the same construction technique. The crews learned this only after the work had been completed. It was a lesson in historical reconstruction.

Even in the aftermath of a devastating fire, the tower remains important due to the number of small communities under its watch. The access to the tower is fairly easy for visitors interested in learning more about the aftermath of the Rodeo-Chediski fire.

Apache Sitgreaves National Forest

Tower: Juniper Ridge
Year Built: 1959
Height: 54'
Manufacture:
  USDA Forest Service
  CL100-106
Model: R-6 flat, 12 x 12 cab
Elevation: 6,998'
District: Lakeside /
  Apache Sitgreaves
Access: Road
Rating: Active

Lake Mountain / Apache Sitgreaves Natl. Forest

Tower: Lake Mountain
Year Built: 1926
Height: 48'
Manufacture:
  Aermotor LX-24 (modified)
Model: 7 x7 cab
Elevation: 8,250'
District:
  Lakeside / Apache-Sitgreaves
Access: Road
Rating: Active

Not all the Forest Service personnel are cut out to be fire lookouts. Jeff Tamietti from the Black Mesa office says he lasted one day. As the afternoon sun warmed the small cab on the Lake Mountain tower, he had reached his limit. He recounts sailing balloons and paper airplanes out of the windows of the tower to fill the slow hours creeping toward sunset. I agree with him: It takes a special person to fill the quiet hours in a seven foot square box!

Lake Mountain

Apache Sitgreaves National Forest

The Forest Service was founded in 1905 and soon began designating mountain peaks as lookout sites for fire watch. When a peak was heavily forested, the watcher might climb a tree to gain a better view of the countryside. In time, the Forest Service built ladders using iron spikes driven into the tree trunks to ease the task of getting to the top for watch. One of these old trees with lag bolts still studding the trunk remains at the top of Lake Mountain. Only the lower half remains standing while the upper half, toppled by a storm, lies in pieces on the ground around the stump. It is a piece of history and visitors can still examine the lag bolts and imagine what it must have been like to climb the tree. Before the tree lost it's top half, one lookout on Lake Mountain climbed to the top. He admits it was a bit scary trusting the old bolts as he rose high above the ground. The lookout tree is across the road from the cabin's porch. It is easy to miss for those unaware of the historical significance of an old snag.

Lake Mountain serves both the northern end of the Fort Apache Reservation as well as Forest Service land that spreads north of McNary and east of Pinetop-Lakeside. To drive through the small community of McNary enroute to the tower is to remember the economic struggle of our native tribes. The poverty of McNary stands in contrast to the higher living standards of the white community ten miles west. It is not uncommon to suddenly confront tribal livestock in the middle of the road just north of town.

As we visited the tower in the late afternoon, we discovered four teenagers from Lakeside who had driven around the barrier and up the narrow road to the summit. It was a beautiful location to gaze at the lakes and forested hills that spread south across the Reservation as the sun set, casting a pink glow in the west. The tower and the small cabin at its base are on the Historic Register. The tower is surrounded by a chain link fence to protect it from vandalism.

O'Haco / Apache Sitgreaves National Forest

Tower: O'Haco
Year Built: 1966
Height: 100'
Manufacture:
  USDA Forest Service

Model: 7 x7 cab
Elevation: 7,640'
District:
  Black Mesa / Apache Sitgreaves
Access: Road
Rating: Active

O'Haco

O'Haco sits in a hole. It has a fine view of Knoll Lake but the neighboring ridges along the horizon limit observation and make it difficult to call in the coordinates of wild fires. The tower has not been staffed since 2001. At least one source, tongue in cheek, says the Forest Service would not be unhappy to see it burn. This is hard to accept with the nice compound below the tower. The hundred foot tower is surrounded by a chain link fence with a cabin near its base. A basketball court and a physical training course are enclosed within the compound. When the tower was in service, an engine crew was stationed at the tower and often used the court or the exercise course to stay in shape. They also ran the stairs of the hundred foot tower. The record for racing up the stairs of the tower was twenty three seconds.

But the tower holds another distinction. The lookout once offered the challenge that no one could sneak up the creaky stairs to take him by surprise. The crews rose to the challenge one afternoon, hauling a fire hose up the stairs, without a squeak giving away their position. Slamming the door of the tower shut and locking off access, they shoved a fire hose through the window and blasted the lookout. It was a humbling moment when he called down to ask permission to change his wet clothes. It gets cold in a tower, soaked to the skin and exposed to the wind above the trees.

Knowing that the tower was not in an optimum position, the Forest Service had a plan to lift the structure out of that location, relocating it to the new Dutch Joe site after that old tower was demolished. They might have made the move all right but the expense of re-certifying the structural soundness of the tower once it was moved proved to be too expensive. The re-location was never made. O'Haco Tower remains overlooking Knoll Lake and is listed as inactive by the Forest Service.

Apache Sitgreaves National Forest

Promontory / Apache Sitgreaves National Forest

Tower: Promontory
Year Built: 1938
Height: 110'
Manufacturer:
 Aermotor LS-40
Model: 7x7 cab
Elevation: 7,931
District: Black Mesa
Access: Road
Rating: Active

Promontory fire tower was originally a wood structure built with poles taken from the forest around the site. The tower proved to be too short for the surrounding forest. In time it was replaced with a metal tower. Construction of the metal tower began inside the wooden frame of the first tower and as the structure crept upward, the crews began dismantling the wood tower, throwing the poles to the ground. The current metal tower at a hundred and ten feet rises twenty feet taller than the old wood tower.

Promontory stands in a wide clearing along FR 300 on the Mogollon Rim. Uninitiated visitors racing along the dusty concourse may be a bit surprised to see the giant rising out of the trees. They may roar past without stopping, speculating about the purpose of the structure. The tower may be one of the easiest to visit though climbing the hundred and ten foot slender stairwell requires a bit of stamina. It receives a high number of visitors due to its location. Visitors climb the steep stairs to see the views from the top and ask the same questions repeatedly. Mike Shore, long time lookout, could answer most of their questions in his sleep.

But there was the day Mike was in the cabin near the tower and vandals crept up the stairs, breaking into the cab, a hundred and ten feet above the ground. They proceeded to throw everything that was detachable out of the cab. Only the fire finder remained as they were unable to maneuver it through the window. Mike arrived in time to find the vandals descending the stairs with his binoculars. He got their license plate number and in time they were apprehended by law enforcement. Mike even got his binoculars back. The tower is now surrounded by a chain link fence topped with barb wire.

Jeff Tamietti at the Black Mesa district office notes that he would prefer the Forest Service facilities have no indication of ownership on their property. The signs seem to serve as an open invitation to vandals to damage the property. It remains a mystery why vandals seem to feel the need to destroy government property as their taxes will ultimately pay the bill to repair the facility. Near the tower is a second site with radio equipment that has remained undamaged possibly due to the lack of signs identifying the facility.

Promontory

Apache Sitgreaves National Forest

PS Knoll / Apache Sitgreaves National Forest

Tower: PS Knoll
Year Built: 1933
Height: 45.9'
Manufacturer: Aermotor LS-39
Model: 7x7 cab
Elevation: 8,045'
District: Alpine / Apache Sitgreaves
Access: Road
Rating: Inactive

PS Knoll

PS Knoll is another 1930's era tower that may have been built by the CCC. The forty-five foot tower has the standard seven foot cab with no catwalk. Across the road from the tower stands a two room cabin as quarters for the lookout with a small storage building and out house behind the cabin.

The tower stands watch over the region south of Big Lake along the East Fork of the Black River. It is a region well watered by annual precipitation that encourages lush vegetation and offers tinder for roaring wild fires.

As we approached the tower, a herd of antelope raced parallel to the road, their speed easily pacing our vehicle. Three elk cows grazed just below the tower.

The tower stands on a knoll cleared of forest growth with no trees to limit the view. The knoll rises out of the center of a large bowl with ridges lining the horizon in two directions. Either the location or budget cuts may account for the fact that the tower is seldom used. It is a site off the beaten path, seldom visited by those who leave columns of dust along the nearby roads. When we visited the tower, the access road was nearly impassable, requiring a short walk up the hillside.

When present, the lookout is responsible for standing watch over the forest west of Highway 191, filling in some of the areas that are not visible to the tower at Big Lake. The tower stands ready for an active fire season when the forest is tinder dry. Its neighboring towers are the Blue which may be decommissioned and Maverick on the White Mountain Apache Reservation.

Apache Sitgreaves National Forest

Reno / Apache Sitgreaves National Forest

Reno Tower overlooks the upper reaches of the Blue Wilderness area as well as the San Carlos Indian Reservation. In reporting fires for two different agencies the Reno lookout can see the differences that exist between federal and tribal fire management due to funding and personnel on site. He pointed to a thin stream of smoke, curling upward on Reservation land.

"I called that in this morning. Looks like they're finally sending someone to check it out," he says with a smile. A column of dust rose from a

Tower: Reno
Year Built: 1965
Height: 54'
Manufacture:
  USDA Forest Service
  CL 100-106

Model: R-6 flat, 12 x 12 cab
Elevation: 9,094'
District: Alpine / Apache Sitgreaves
Access: Road
Rating: Active

dirt road hidden by the trees. "They have a different agenda. It takes them a bit longer to jump on these things. There may be a boundary line out there but fire does not respect man-made boundaries. If the tribe fails to control a fire on their side of the line, the flames may jump to the Forest Service land and it becomes a multi-agency fire."

Two months later I met the Geronimo Hot Shots based on the San Carlos Reservation. They take a great deal of pride in their work and are eager to respond to the smoke sightings. At the beginning of the season they had jumped on every hot spot. But as the season heated up, they were frequently called out of state. This left a skeleton crew to deal with the hot spots. The Reno lookout didn't know this and the response left him frustrated as he watched the column of smoke increase.

I asked about aerial recon for the region. The flights depend on the weather. They are useful to help guide the crews into fires but the lookout struggles to coordinate the location as his reference points may differ from the observers in the air. He noted that smoke jumpers may work well up in the remote regions of Idaho and Montana where there are few roads across the wilderness. They may not be the best solution for Arizona. He talked about the length of time it takes to assemble the crew and check weather forecasts and wind conditions. He has watched as the airplane arrived on site and began to circle the smoke, dropping streamers to check wind direction and speed. Each pass took time and after two jumpers dropped on the fire and were blown off course, the pilot backed off to wait for better conditions. In the time the preparation took, it might have been faster to send a crew to the location by ground.

Along with his duties as a lookout, he leaves water out for his neighbors, the wild animals, that pass through his clearing. He talked about the grouse and turkey, the bear, deer and elk, showing a deep respect for the forest and wildlife surrounding the tower.

Regarding the job as lookout, he says "people who live in lookout towers really have to like themselves!"

Reno

Apache Sitgreaves National Forest

Rose Peak / Apache Sitgreaves National Forest

A narrow, two lane strip of asphalt winds through the Blue Range Wilderness, along ridges parallel to the Arizona - New Mexico border. It is a remote area with a few scattered settlements and isolated ranches. The terrain drops from deeply carved ridges covered with ponderosa pine down into the juniper and scrub oak transition zone. To make a point about the sparse population, the lookout at Rose Peak points down to Eagle Creek with a little one room schoolhouse. The school once held a dozen students. Now just two students remain, both home schooled.

Highway 191 bisects the Blue Range Wilderness. Driving south from Alpine down to the mining communities of Clifton - Morenci, sightseers may only pass a half dozen cars in two hours of peeling through constant turns. In such a remote area, the lookout on Rose Peak takes on an important role, beyond spotting fires, in assisting stranded motorists or those caught

Tower: Rose Peak
Year Built: 1981
Height: 21'
Manufacture: US Forest Service
Model: D-1, 14 x 14 cab

Elevation: 8,786'
District: Clifton /
   Apache Sitgreaves
Access: Road & Trail
Rating: Active

in horrific accidents. An ambulance might take two hours to reach an accident near Rose Peak. A call from the lookout can bring an air rescue helicopter much sooner and possibly save a life.

The district only sees about thirty-five fires in an average fire season. The lookout speculates that the juniper may be slower to catch from a lightening strike. She does remember one particular fire that began with a controlled burn near Rose Peak. The wind soon swept the flames over the road intended as a fire break. Laughing, she says she was out of there long before the flames crept up the little hill toward the tower.

The current tower is one story, with a spacious fourteen foot square cab, built in 1981. It replaced a wood tower built in 1929. Nearby a two room cabin is home for the lookout. In the early days, a family of skunks lived beneath the cabin. It was a challenging time when lightening flashed and the skunks would get a bit excited, leaving the cabin reeking of scent.

Working ten days on, four days off, the lookout may return with a road sign to post along Highway 191. It is a long way across the district and she is not adverse to helping out the road crews as her husband oversees the region for ADOT.

As we talk, she points out the smoke from a fire near Escudilla Peak and then a second white cloud rising above the horizon. She called the second cloud a water dog. It is a term I hear repeatedly from other lookouts indicating a cumulus type cloud structure, similar to a column of smoke, building out of water vapor rising above the earth's surface. Beginners frequently call these in - a bogus call, something no lookout wants to do. As with other lookouts, she prefers the active times. Lightening storms are her least favorite part of the job. She stands on her stool with its glass insulators, turns off the radio and waits, not daring to touch anything. She says her "heart ends up in her throat."

Along with the Blue Wilderness and the Blue River, the tower overlooks the San Carlos Apache Reservation to the west and Steeple Rock in New Mexico further east.

Rose Peak

Apache Sitgreaves National Forest

Springer Mountain / Apache Sitgreaves N. F.

Tower: Springer Mountain
Year Built: 1933
Height: 31'
Manufacture: Aermotor MC-24
Model: L-4, 12 x 12 cab

Elevation: 7,203'
District:
　Lakeside / Apache-Sitgreaves
Access: Road
Rating: Active

Springer Mountain is an urban tower. The access road winds through a small neighborhood, up a forested hillside, breaking out on the peak, to look over the small town below. The tower, like so many others, is surrounded by chain link fence, topped with barb wire. It is a reminder of vandals that move out from our cities to destroy public property.

The tower is easily visible from State Route 260 as it passes through the communities of Lakeside, Pinetop and Showlow. In turn, Jane Croxen, the lookout, can witness rush hour on SR260 from a bird's eye view. House fires may be reported along with the wildfires out in the forest. She may even report trash burning when a resident has forgotten to file for a permit.

In being so close to town, she sees a lot of visitors, on average one person per hour. Like other lookouts, she has the option of closing the door when business pulls her attention away from answering the questions of curious visitors. The road to the tower serves as a focal point for hikers and runners who are out for a bit of exercise, some visiting Jane on a regular basis. She does not grow lonesome for lack of company.

It is a world apart from the life her grandfather, Fred Croxen, experienced as one of Arizona's first lookouts. He stood watch on Woody Mountain near Flagstaff, beginning in either 1911 or 1912. At the turn of the century, the region around Flagstaff had been clear cut by the logging industry. As the trees returned to the site, the Forest Service hired Fred to stand watch on Woody Mountain. He packed in supplies by horseback.

Unlike her grandfather, Jane has all the modern conveniences with a car that will take her up the steep slope in a matter of minutes and electricity to light the tower and power the radio. Jane is continuing the family tradition that started when modern industry first staked a foothold in the western United States.

The Springer Mountain tower is covered with siding, giving it a more modern appearance. It was built in 1933, the era of the CCC. Due to the remodeling, it is not eligible for the National Historic Register.

Springer Mountain

Apache Sitgreaves National Forest

Former Towers / Apache Sitgreaves Nat'l. Forest

The Story of Dutch Joe

This one hundred foot wood tower once stood on private land but has since been demolished by the Forest Service. The struggle that the old wooden tower put up against demolition leaves one to ask why it wasn't restored to prime condition.

The old tower, built with heavy beams, was surrounded by a catwalk. At the base of the tower was a small two room cabin and outhouse. An underground cistern was dug next to the cabin. The cabin was well loved and well cared for by the couple who lived there. The woman was an artist who painted glow-in-the-dark artwork in the outhouse, possibly for perusal during late night forays to the little building. In the mid 1980's, the stairway up Dutch Joe began to deteriorate. The catwalk creaked ominously when the lookout strolled around the cab. Lookouts took special care to descend backward down the steep top flight. There was no money in the budget to fix the tower and so it was closed. The tower was located on private land and word of the situation reached the absentee land owner. She was concerned about the liability to visitors. Would a visitor attempt to reach the upper level, fall, be injured or even killed in the process?

The Forest Service agreed to demolish the tower though it was one of the best locations for a lookout as it covered a lot of territory. Wrecking crews moved onto the site and began by digging out the cistern. They shoved the old cabin into the hole created by the cistern and then covered it. Next they turned their attention to Dutch Joe. It was too solid to be pushed over so they loosened the guy wires and supports. They piled a large amount of tinder against the supporting logs and spread a gel guaranteed to burn over the structure and the tinder. Then using a flame thrower they inundated the pile with flame. The tinder burned to ash. Dutch Joe stood unperturbed. They added fuel to the fire and still the tower stood. The crews grew frustrated but still laughed at their dilemma. Here was a tower that had been declared unsafe and yet it would not surrender to a flame thrower with fuel to burn. Finally the crews used bulldozers to pull the tower down and burned the remains. They did not, as told in popular myth, use dynamite. It may have occurred to them but no one was licensed to use dynamite and these were law-abiding forest rangers. Frustrated but law abiding. Dutch Joe lost the battle to stand and has never been rebuilt at a new location. It was simply too expensive to move another tower onto the site even though the current towers do not have the panorama offered by Dutch Joe. Other lookouts complain that they once used the tower to help them judge distance on the columns of smoke. Dutch Joe is sorely missed.

Former Towers

Antelope Mountain/TV Knoll
Year Built: 1950's
Height: 5'
Manufacture: Modified popcorn stand
Model: Metal cabin
Elevation: 9,003'
District: Alpine

Chevelon Butte
Year Built: 1928
Height: 3'
Manufacture: Forest Service
Model: Cabin
Elevation: 6,945'
District: Black Mesa

Gobbler Point
Report of site but no further information.

Pat Knoll
Year Built: 1914
Height: 38'
Manufacture: Forest Service
Model: Crow's Nest
Elevation: 9,661'
District: Springerville

Williams Valley
Year Built: possibly 1920's
Height: unknown
Manufacture: Forest Service
Model: Crow's Nest
Elevation: 9273"
District: Alpine

Apache Sitgreaves National Forest

Rodeo-Chediski Fire

Two fires, set by two people, caused nearly 500,00 acres of forest devastation. Two people: one, a woman, lost, alone with no training in wilderness survival; the other a trained fire fighter with a need for employment. Each set a fire for their own survival.

To the horror of Arizona residents, the two fires totalling over 235,000 acres, merged. From June 18 to July 7, 2002, the fires burned 462,614 acres along with 426 structures. It cost approximately $153 million dollars to fight what became known as the Rodeo-Chediski fire.

What has not been discussed is the impact on the fire towers that overlooked this region. Five of the state's towers were directly impacted by the inferno, more than by any one fire at one time in the history of the state. Five years later, the region burned by the fire is just starting to see enough recovery to justify bringing two of the towers back on line. One will be used only as needed. Two towers have remained in service though their territories were severely burned.

The Rodeo fire began near the Rodeo fairgrounds outside Cibique on the Fort Apache Reservation. A fire fighter, out of work and hoping to gain employment, set a small fire. In talking with forest service personnel, I have learned that this is not that uncommon. Dry, hot, windy conditions, caused the fire to spread beyond control.

That first night the White Mountain Apaches threw their fire crews into action. As I talked with the lookout who had been working a fire tower that summer, he proudly related how the crews had fought the fire to a stand still, repeating, "They almost caught it. They almost held it." The next day as temperatures rose with the rising sun, the fire exploded and began its run north.

Two days later, a young woman stranded with a vendor's broken down truck walked up a hill and lost her way in the dense forest. Wandering through the ponderosa, she panicked. She convinced herself that no one would find her unless she started a fire to catch the attention of one of the aircraft flying toward the Rodeo fire fifteen miles to the west. Ignoring the high winds and tinder dry conditions, she lit fire to a bush which rapidly exploded out of control. She did catch the attention of a helicopter crew that rescued her but started a second major forest fire. Crews working the Rodeo fire were sent to try to surround the Chediski but with forest and weather conditions, it proved to be impossible. The fires merged and began the inevitable march north toward the communities lining State Route 260.

Limestone Tower was the first to be impacted with flames roaring up the ridges below the tower. Flying over the site, one can see the line just below the tower where the flames stood on three sides, before turning away. On one side a grove of green trees still stands, the green flowing down the hillside away from the tower. This is seemingly impossible in the utter devastation on the remaining three quarters surrounding the tower. Enough brush remains that the tower is still being used.

Chediski was next. Visit the tower now and one drives through a forest of giant burnt matchsticks. The tower stands above it all on a high ridge. There are still a few green trees mixed with the black totems in a mosaic pattern near the tower but the region is devastated. The tower is currently not manned or used.

The fire crews of the Apache-Sitgreaves National Forest knew the fires were coming but were powerless to stop the flames. Each day, fire tech Jeff Tamietti would drive along Forest Road 300 between the Gentry and Deer Springs fire towers monitoring the movement of the fire. He assigned crews to begin thinning the forests around each tower. It is standard practice to create a zone sixty-five feet in diameter around a structure to protect it from the fire. For Deer Spring, sitting on a rocky ridge, surrounded by cobblestone, this was sufficient. But with Gentry, the forest had closed in around the tower, leaving a potential Roman torch. The crews worked a hundred and twenty foot diameter around the tower, clearing out brush and small trees with the hope of saving the structure.

Forest Road 300 follows the Mogollon Rim, a natural rampart rising two thousand feet above the valleys below. It was a natural break in the green canopy. From the rim, one can see for miles across unbroken forest. It was a natural place to watch the advance of the flames. The crews had hoped to use FR300 as a fire break when the flames came over the rim. The canyons that cut into the rim funneled the flames upward, creating a superheated updraft. The flames jumped FR 300 without pause.

Fire crews fell back toward the communities of Showlow, Linden, Pinedale, Clay Springs, Heber and Forest Lakes prepared to make a final stand. They had no time to think about Gentry, Deer Springs and Juniper Ridge towers.

Rodeo-Chediski Fire

Apache-Sitgreaves National Forest

Rodeo - Chediski Fire Map

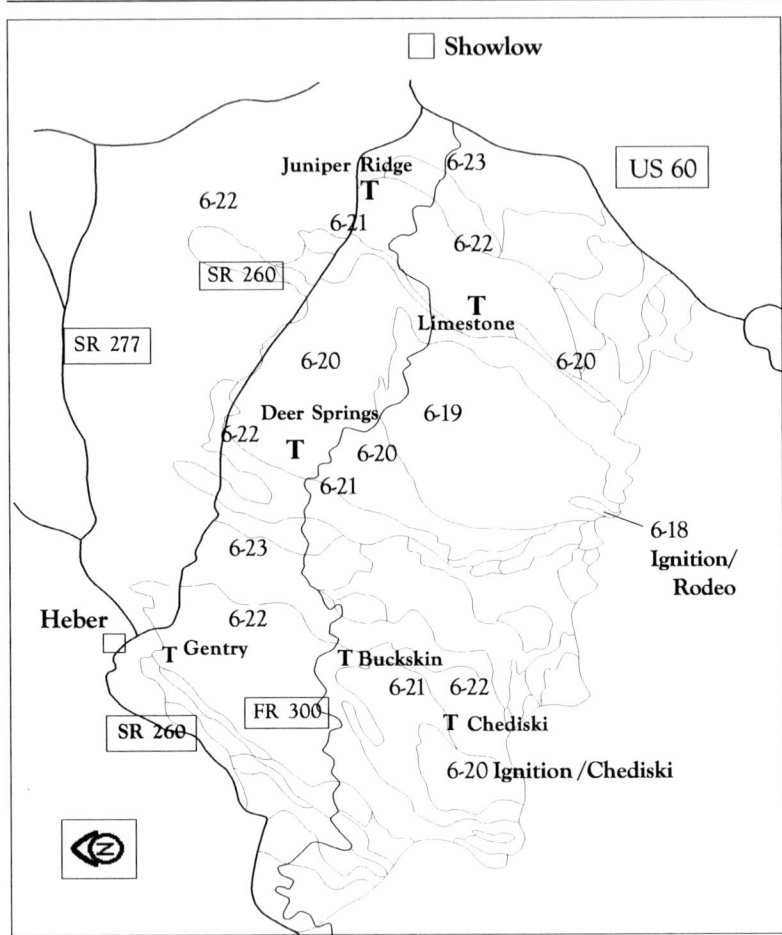

Map is intended to show locations of fire towers and the dates those areas burned in order to understand the impact on the fire towers and how quickly this fire consumed such a large region. All other areas burned between June 24 - July 1. Map available from the Apache Sitgreaves National Forest.

Juniper Ridge below the tower was possibly the most effected of the three towers. Almost no trees remain on the ridge though grass has returned to hold the soil against the rains. Standing at the base of the tower, a visitor's eyes are drawn to the northeast, to the community of Showlow. The tower still has a community to protect though most of the forest south of the structure is gone.

Both Deer Springs and Gentry still stand in green trees. Did the thinning around each tower help? Probably but by this point the fire was burning in more of a mosaic pattern than it had through much of area further south and east. While Gentry remained in service, Deer Springs has been used only by fire crews on a temporary basis.

In the end, the flames reached the outer edges of the communities, leaving a wake of thousands of acres of torched forest and brush. For visitors driving along State Route 260, lined by the skeletons of burned ponderosa, the impact of the massive wildfire begins to set in. I've seen the blackened remnants of old burns in the forest, a few acres with green grasses sprouting around what remains of blackened trunks. This is beyond anything that we have seen before in Arizona. But it is only when I took to the air in a small plane that the full impact of these fires really settled in. Flying over the blackened hills, the scars of the fire reach to the horizon, the dead trees beyond count. It is impossible to fully comprehend the impact that will stretch for decades, possibly centuries, before the forest is restored to its former grandeur.

The towers survived. The lookouts are working again as brush, and in limited areas, small trees begin to sprout. In some canyons, the terrain is a moonscape, even the earth scorched. In other areas, the fire burned a mosaic pattern, leaving some stands of trees untouched while destroying others. With the dry winter of 2005, grass stood knee high, untouched by deep snow. In 2006, the lookouts watched for that thin stream of smoke that will send crews scrambling to the next fire along dirt roads, racing against time.

Fort Apache Reservation

Chapter 8

The Fort Apache Reservation is the ancestral home of the White Mountain Apache. The tribal headquarters are at White River, south of Pinetop-Lakeside. The reservation spreads over 1.6 million acres with the elevation rising from 3,000 feet to 11,403 feet at Mt Baldy. Established in 1891, the Fort Apache Indian Reservation encompassed both the San Carlos and the White Mountain Apaches on one reservation. In 1897, the Reservation was split into two distinct entities. Sometimes the tribe speak well of each other, at other times a bit of rivalry is evident.

The 12,000 members of the White Mountain Apaches are spread over eleven major communities. This is a bit different from the neighboring Navajo tribe. The Navajos frequently retain individual home sites across reservation lands while many of the Apaches live in communities, allowing their scenic lands to be used for recreation, benefitting the entire tribe. The Apaches have pursued economic interests in tourism, recreation, logging and most recently, the casino at Hondah.

The Fort Apache Reservation is lushly forested with some of the most beautiful land in Arizona, including both the Black and Salt Rivers. Small lakes open to recreation dot reservation lands. The Sunrise Ski Area in the northeast corner of the reservation is one of four ski resorts in the state.

Six towers stand watch over the forest, three remain in service. In 2002, the Rodeo-Chediski Fire devastated large portions of the forest on the Fort Apache Reservation, creating an economic challenge to the tribal logging industry. It will be many decades before the land recovers and the tribe benefits again from the charred acres.

Like their neighbors to the south, the White Mountain Apaches send highly respected hot shot crews across the western United States. The Fort Apache reservation shares a border with the Tonto, the Apache Sitgreaves and the San Carlos Reservations. Portions of the Apache lands are closed to non-Apaches requiring that visitors check their travel plans with the Tribe before visiting the Reservation.

Buckskin / Fort Apache Reservation

Tower: Buckskin
Year Built: 1963
Height: 82.6'
Manufacture: International Derrick
Model: 7 x 7 cab
Elevation: 6,480'
District: Fort Apache Tribe
Access: Road
Rating: Inactive

Buckskin

Fort Apache Reservation

Three towers, including Buckskin, stand on the Fort Apache Reservation along the Mogollon rim, south of FR 300. Before the Rodeo-Chediski fire, Buckskin was used infrequently when dry conditions left the forest a tinder box.. Even with Chediski no longer used on a full-time basis due to the fire, Buckskin continues to be designated as inactive.

Buckskin is located on a part of the Reservation that is off limits to non-Apaches unless accompanied by an employee of the tribe. En route to the towers, we passed a patrol vehicle, assigned to keep out non-residents. Noting the .45 caliber pistol clipped to the belt of one man, I realized that they take this assignment seriously. Randall filled in the details, describing incidents that have occurred in the restricted zone. Buckskin is not a location for drop-in visitors.

Like many of the sites, this tower, with its little cabin, is in poor condition. Yet the location set among mature ponderosa pine is beautiful with extensive views off the rim. We walked to the base of the tower, to look up at the structure, one of the few from International Derrick. It appears very similar to the Aermotor towers. The gate in the perimeter fence was locked.

Before leaving, I examined the small cabin near the tower. Two of the windows were broken. Grafitti covered the walls inside. The cabin had not been occupied in a long time. Glancing at the roof, I realized that it was covered with stamped metal shingles laid in sheets across the surface. A narrow spine ran the length of the roof with an ornamental knob at each end. It was an elegant accent despite the slovenly conditions of the rooms below.

As we stood below the tower, Randall, one of my Apache guides, pointed to a cloud burst obscuring a distant ridge. "That's Limestone over there," he told me. I asked if the rain would be a problem. "That road is really bad when it gets wet", he informed me. We agreed to give it a try with the option of turning back if the road proved to be bad.

I should have recognized what Randall was telling me. Thirty minutes later, with mud slinging against the wheel wells, I realized that my desire to personally visit each of the towers might have to wait for another day. (see page 160)

Chediski / Fort Apache Reservation

Three years after the fire, Chediski sits on a lonely peak, out of service among the black sentinels of burned trees. As we approached the tower, a band of wild horses broke through the trees, running from our truck. A white stallion turned to challenge us as his band made their way across the hillside.

Chediski and Limestone are two of the tallest towers in the state at one hundred-twenty feet on top of a concrete base. Regardless of my fear of heights, I was determined to climb this tower. My escort climbed ahead of me, only to stop eighty feet above the ground. "Think you can make it across here?" he asked. I looked up at a platform with only one board remaining across an empty span, the thin air framed by metal supports. I couldn't believe that I was contemplating stepping onto an eight-inch span of weathered wood to reach the next set of stairs. I told him I would make it and took a firmer grip

Tower: Chediski
Year Built: 1936
Height: 120'
Manufacture:
  Aermotor MC-99
Model: 7 x 7 cab
Elevation: 7,462'
District: Fort Apache Tribe
Access: Road
Rating:
  Inactive till area recovers

on the handrail as I gingerly set my weight on the narrow board. I tried very hard not to think about the eighty feet of empty air below me as I made the turn to the next flight. We reached the top and found that the lock had been changed. There was no access to the tower cab. As we made our way back down I faced an empty square of blue sky where a platform once stood. The boards of the platform littered the ground below. I focused on seeing only the eight inch board, concentrated on stepping on just that board. It was just eighty feet of open air.

A modern cabin stands near the tower, its windows covered with decorative metal work. We peered inside at neatly painted walls and an abandoned refrigerator. Randall told me that no one lived here when the tower was manned as it was regarded as unsafe. Rattlesnakes live under the house and the bathroom facilities are unsanitary. Instead the lookout lived in a small cabin nearby. It burned when the Chediski fire ran over the peak. The tower survived, its cab floor and platforms intact.

A large clearing to one side serves as a helispot with a small shelter at the edge of the landing area. A large water tank sits on a platform behind the cabin.

The tower overlooks the western side of the reservation, the view stretching to Four Peaks and along the Mogollon Rim. It is spectacular even with black totems spread across the hillside. Mexican locus are spreading quickly to cover the burned slopes. Randall told me they are beginning to replant some of the areas burned by the fire. He demonstrated a tool that is twisted like a post hole digger, quickly leaving a hole for each little seedling. I asked Sam, a lookout, if the height didn't bother him the first time he climbed the tower.

"Sure it bothered me. The first time it got windy, that tower started rocking and I came down to check the bolts to see if they were holding tight," he said.

Randall started laughing at the thought of the tower flying off the peak with Sam holding onto the metal frame like a hang glider. Sam just smiled and followed the road off the peak. I glanced back at the tower framed by blackened tree trunks. It seemed so lonely, so desolate.

Chediski

Fort Apache Reservation

Limestone / Fort Apache Reservation

Limestone and its sister tower, Chediski, overlook the western half of the Apache Reservation. They each stand one hundred twenty-feet high, from the concrete slab to the base of their cabs. They are the highest towers in the state. That is one hundred-twenty feet of open stairway, flight after flight, rising through the atmosphere with only a thin hand rail between the lookout and a long fall to earth. It has been recommended that the Apaches enclose the

Tower: Limestone
Year Built: 1936
Height: 120'
Manufacture: Aermotor MC-99
Model: 7 x 7 cab
Elevation: 7,105'
District: Fort Apache Tribe
Access: Road
Rating: Active

stairs with waist high chain link. In 2006, this had yet to be completed.

There is little to compare to standing a hundred feet above the ground, surrounded by a couple of inches of angle iron, with nothing else to contain one in thin air. In climbing, the tower, it is better to keep one's attention on the horizon rather than the narrow board beneath one's feet.

Unable to reach the Limestone tower by road due to deep mud, I flew over the site. The full impact of the Rodeo-Chediski fire was evident as the small plane flew over mile after mile of burnt totems rising from the scarred earth. Approaching the tower from the east, we could see a line of blackened trees along the ridge just short of the tower where the fire line held. On three sides around the tower, the fire has wiped out an entire forest. A green grove of ponderosa pine rises to one side as a reminder of what is gone. A small cabin also remains at the foot of the tower. Due to the growth of brush, the downed trees and the remaining forest in one sector below Limestone, the tower is still manned.

One of the pilots pointed to a canyon below us. "That's Hop Canyon. If the fire had gone up Hop canyon, Showlow would have been gone," he repeatedly told me.

I glanced across the horizon at the little community and asked him how far we were from Showlow. He told me it was ten miles. Hop Canyon runs on a north-south axis, a direct chute toward Showlow, full of fuel for the advancing flames. Ten miles seemed like a long way but with the flames roaring through the canopy, hot spots breaking out in advance of the fire line, it would not have taken long for the fire to devour the town. It is a credit to the fire crews that fought to save the community.

Both the pilots from the anglo community of Showlow as well as the Apaches told me that more work needs to be done on the remaining Reservation forests. They have not been thinned as needed the last few years. It is a tinder box awaiting a spark. The lookouts have their work set before them, peering through binoculars at each faint sign of smoke.

Limestone

Fort Apache Reservation

163

The Road to Limestone

Limestone Fire Tower was one of the tribe's active towers in 2002, before the Rodeo-Chediski conflagration. We never made it to Limestone tower by road. As two Forestry employees and I drove along FR 300 toward the tower, rain drops spattered against the windshield. Earlier, as we drove out of the Fort Apache dispatch center, Randall unequivocally stated that he wanted to sing in Apache but if he did it would rain. As the raindrops grew larger, Sam peered at him from behind dark glasses. "You been sitting there humming all this time, haven't you?" Randall laughed and we all looked at the rain drops on the windshield.

Sam stopped along the road to point out the tower on a distant ridge, a tiny silhouette rising above the trees. I silently wondered if he wished that the distant image would satisfy me and not require him to drive out to Limestone. As he resumed driving, I concentrated on asking him questions about the work of the Apache Hot Shot crews. Gradually I became aware of the mud spinning off the tires to pound the inside of the wheel wells. Glancing at the road surface ahead of the truck, I was confused. The surface appeared to be firm, no sign of mud and yet the sound increased.

Soon the back end of the truck began to sway slightly. I glanced up, unable to concentrate on my laptop. Setting it aside, I focused on the road. The truck was obviously fishtailing by this point with Sam maintaining a light touch on the wheel. It slid toward the ditch on the right side as Sam steered into the skid, pulling the truck back toward the center of the road. Not once or twice but repeatedly he pulled the truck back into line. But the moment came when his skill could no longer pull us around and we traveled the road sideways, sliding ever near the ditch.

Randall muttered, "Sam, four wheel drive."

Sam fought the wheel.

Randall's hands fluttered over his knee. "Sam, four wheel drive!"

The truck teetered on the edge of the ditch as Sam fumbled for the lever at floor level and then we shuddered to a stop, the front wheels firmly planted in the ditch, the truck sideways across the road. Outwardly I remained calm as I thought of us all out in the mud, sliding and struggling to push the heavy truck out of the ditch. I wondered how far we would have to walk to reach town. Both Sam and Randall giggled as Sam studied the lever in his hand for the correct gear.

"What do you think? Four low?" asked Sam.

Still laughing, Randall said, "You ignored me when I said four wheel drive and put us in the ditch. Now you want to know what I think?"

Sam shifted into four low and the truck shuddered as all four wheels struggled against the heavy clay, finally turning, fighting for traction. We stayed in the ditch, covering ground until it leveled out with the road and we climbed back to the middle of the track. We all breathed a sigh of relief and Sam continued to fishtail along the muddy surface.

Hesitant to question their knowledge of the road, I still suggested we didn't need to make Limestone. We could turn back. Sam continued down the road, no comment.

Again I reminded them that we agreed we would turn back if it got ugly. Randall then told me that a turnoff was just up the road and it would be easier to make for that road than to turn back along the route we had just come over.

Relieved, I listened as Randall and Sam continued to tease each other about Sam's driving and his determination to avoid four wheel drive as long as possible. It was obvious that each respected the other. Randall turned back in his seat to tell me that he preferred to let Sam do the driving. And for my part I was thankful that Sam was an excellent driver in deep mud. To make his point, Randall explained that if we tried to go to Limestone, we would face mud nearly ten inches deep on the road surface. We were all relieved to see the turn off ahead that would take us to Pinetop.

I thought I might make another attempt to reach Limestone when it dried out. Or maybe I could find a photo in the archives, certainly better choices than walking miles to the nearest town through deep mud.

The Road to Limestone

Maverick / Fort Apache Reservation

Maverick Fire Tower stands on the eastern edge of the Fort Apache Reservation, overlooking the Mt. Baldy Wilderness, Gobbler Point, Chiricahua Butte and the north edge of the San Carlos Apache Reservation. To reach the tower, we drove the old road through a narrow canyon, up the back side of Maverick Peak. The floor of the canyon only had room for a rough two-wheeled track that followed a sparkling mountain stream. We stopped at a small waterfall for a drink of water while Sam described an encounter with an alpino bull elk on the steep, densely forested slope above us. It is a long drive over dirt roads from the headquarters at White River.

It is not uncommon for the Maverick or Odart Towers to call in cross readings for the fires on the San Carlos Reservation. They also note fires

Tower: Maverick Mountain
Year Built: 1934
Height: 82.6'
Manufacture: Aermotor MC-39
Model: 7 x 7 cab
Elevation: 8,086'
District: Fort Apache Tribe
Access: Road
Rating: Active

on the Apache-Sitgreaves National Forest. Above the tree tops it is hard to distinguish exactly where one agency's authority ends and another begins.

Sam, one of my Apache guides, had been the lookout at Chediski when the fire first broke out. After the fires were extinguished, he transferred to the Maverick tower. To break the monotony of working on the tower, he reads or runs up and down the stairs for exercise. He does a bit of carpentry repairing the tower. In the off season, he doesn't miss the long days in a 7 x 7 cab. He enjoys the chance to do something a bit different each week.

As we stood in Maverick Tower, I noted the bullet holes through the walls, up through the ceiling. Sam assured me they occur during the off season when he is not in the tower. Vandalism seems to be as big a problem on the reservation as in the National Forest.

He has spent time working with the Apache Hot Shots and with BIA maintenance. The maintenance work first brought him into contact with the towers, creating an interest in the job. After applying it took another three years before an opening allowed him to move up the ladder as lookout. He enjoys the opportunity to help coordinate the work of fire crews and helicopters with the dispatch center. He radios information about what roads will lead into the fire and what resources are required to fight the blaze. The dispatchers then pass it to the fire crews.

Driving to the tower, he has encountered some of the non-native visitors to this part of the reservation, stopping to help with a flat tire or re-unite lost parties. He talked a lot about hunting and told me that after the fire, the cleanup crews found a lot of dead elk along the roads. But the most haunting story is from a firefighter who watched a bull elk and two cows along with two wild horses take refuge in a canyon as the flames approached. The canyon did not have an exit at the far end and the fire swept up the canyon. The elk and horses never came out. We each quietly ponder the desperate fate of animals who do not understand the fire threatening their homes - another reason so stand watch.

Maverick

Fort Apache Reservation

167

McKay Peak / Fort Apache Reservation

McKay was the first fire tower built on the Fort Apache Reservation, dating back to 1932 in the CCC era. The tower overlooks Hawley Lake as well as Pinetop-Lakeside, the East Fork of the Black River, the Mt. Baldy Wilderness and the eastern half of the reservation. The views seen through the low, multi-paned windows on a cool cloudy morning are beyond compare. Mountain ranges fade to the horizon with small lakes scattered across the country. Tall pines and aspen compete for sunlight in the dense forest.

Below the tower stands a two-room cabin in poor repair. As the commute is fairly short, the lookouts do not live in the cabin. A second storage building stands nearby. The peak has several communications towers.

Tower: McKay Peak
Year Built: 1932
Height: 31.6'
Manufacture: Aermotor MC-24
Model: L-4
Elevation: 9,171'
District: Fort Apache Tribe
Access: Road
Rating: Active

As it sits close to a popular lake, the tower receives a lot of visitors. The three flights are not as a daunting as with some of the taller towers on the reservation. The lookout at McKay spends more time educating the public about his responsibilities than other lookouts on the Reservation.

Unlike the Aermotor towers on peaks across the Reservation, this cab is spacious and the lower ledge of the windows do not rise much above the knee, leaving the feeling one could simply step out, walking on air toward the distant peaks. Unfortunately, the structure is showing its age.

McKay is the relay point for many of the mobile units working in the area as it sits above a natural bowl that contains Hawley Lake. Crews working down toward the lake may find limited reception, thus relying on the lookout at McKay Peak to relay their calls to the dispatch center.

As we stood, looking out over the forest, Sam recalled one lively afternoon at McKay Peak. A lightening storm had moved in and was striking throughout the north end of the Reservation. The McKay Peak lookout called in one fire after another, all caused by lightening strikes. In the other towers, the lookouts could only listen and wish that they were there, that it was their turn to share in the adrenalin rush.

McKay Peak

Inside McKay Tower, looking southwest across Fort Apache Reservation.

Fort Apache Reservation

Odart / Fort Apache Reservation

Tower: Odart
Year Built: 1934
Height: 82.6'
Manufacture: Aermotor MC-39
Model: 7 x 7 cab
Elevation: 8,525'
District: Fort Apache Tribe
Access: Road   Rating: Active

As I climbed the stairs of Odart Tower, the width of each platform beneath me shrank in size. What had been broad wood beam platforms became, narrow pocket size turning points. I concentrated on the horizon, ignoring the increasing distance between the platforms and the ground.

The tower stands watch over Long Tom Canyon, Marshall Butte and the Mount Baldy wilderness. Below the tower, forested ridges march off to the horizon, a reminder of the isolation of these towers, tiny specks in a sea of forest.

That sense of isolation was reflected in a unique piece of artwork inked on the back of the board that supports the map for the topography below. A majestic elk, it's antlers spreading wide across the wood grain stares out at the lookout who created it's image in the quiet moments of his watch. I commented on what a fine job the artist, Reece Peaches, has done. Sam dug out another piece of artwork that had been silk screened on their t-shirts by the same artist. It shows a set of binoculars focused on a stream of smoke with a slogan saying "smoke will not escape their eyes". It is not uncommon for lookouts to develop their talent in art or in craft work while standing watch.

At the base of the tower a small trailer holds radio equipment and supplies for fire crews. As I walked around the site, the men checked that all was in order. The heliopad was covered with bright wild flowers and tall grasses. During the warmer months, a fire truck may be stationed at the site, waiting for the next smoke report.

Odart

Fort Apache Reservation

Odart Elk
Pen & Ink
Artist:
Reece Peaches

Former Towers / Fort Apache Reservation

Bonita Rock
Year Built: 1920's
Height: 8'
Manufacture:
  White Mountain Apache IR
Model: Wood Cabin
Elevation: 8,600'
Reservation: Fort Apache

Cerro Gordo
Year Built: 1939
Height: 67.6'
Manufacture: Aermotor LS-40
Model: 7 x 7' cab
Elevation: 9,161'
Reservation: Fort Apache

Faught Ridge
Year Built: 1935
Height: 99.9'
Manufacture: Aermotor MC-39
Model: 7 x 7 cab
Elevation: 7,021'
Reservation: Fort Apache

Kinney Butte
Year Built: 1936
Height: 120'
Manufacture:
  possibly Aermotor MC-99
Model: 7 x 7' cab
Elevation: 8,270'
Reservation: Fort Apache

Mount Baldy
Year Built: 1936
Height: 1'
Manufacture: Forest Service
Model: Six-sided cabin
Elevation: 11,404'
Reservation: Fort Apache

Round Top Mountain
Year Built: 1938
Height: 30'
Manufacture: Aermotor MC-24
Model: L-4 cab
Elevation: 7,189'
Reservation: Fort Apache

San Carlos Apache Reservation

Chapter 9

The San Carlos Apache Reservation may be best known for the San Carlos Reservoir, a lake that once drew fishermen throughout the southwest. The reservation was established in 1871 and spreads over 1.8 million acres. It is the largest of the Apache reservations in the state, sharing a border with the Fort Apache Reservation to the north. It is not uncommon for lookouts for the two tribes to cross each other's smoke sighting, requiring lookouts to know the terrain of both reservations. The reservation also includes the Black River and Salt River Recreational areas, both well appreciated by outdoor enthusiasts. The San Carlos also shares a border with the Apache Sitgreaves National Forest.

Many visitors to San Carlos and Talkalai Lakes remain unaware of the beautifully forested lands in the northeastern section of the reservation known as Point of Pines. From Route 70, a paved highway crosses desert flatland to a dramatic climb along soaring cliffs of the Natanes Plateau. Pullouts offer extended views of the desert plain below. In entering Point of Pines, visitors seemed to have entered a different world from the desolate flats below.

The San Carlos Apaches currently have two towers, one on each end of the reservation. One tower stands watch over Point of Pines while a second tower watches the region surrounding the tribal headquarters at San Carlos. Hilltop, the second, is one of the few desert lookout sites in the state.

The San Carlos is also home to the Geronimo Hot Shots, a level one fire crew, known throughout the country as one of the top fire fighting teams. When the Apaches arrive at a fire, they are highly respected for their skills. It is an honor in the close-knit social structure of the Reservation to be chosen to serve with the team. It is also one of the best opportunities for employment on the financially challenged Reservation.

Dry Lake / San Carlos Apache Reservation

Tower: Dry Lake
Year Built: 1984
Height: 80'
Manufacture: undetermined

Model: 7 x 7 cab
Elevation: 7,484'
Access: Road
Rating: Active

Dry Lake

Visitors drive through the unrelieved glare on Route 70 across the San Carlos Apache Reservation, hoping for a glimpse of cool water in San Carlos Lake. Those who turn onto Apache Route 8 are rewarded by a startling climb up the side of the Natanes Plateau into the restful green of Point of Pines. Who would have guessed that such a beautiful pocket exists above the dry plains of the Gila Valley? I passed a massive elk along the road, its antlers gleaming in the late afternoon light. It is a treasure worth protecting with the fire tower that stands above Dry Lake. When I visited, Dry Lake was a sparkling body of water populated with dead standing tree trunks leaving me uncertain about how the lake got its name.

Dry Lake fire tower stands on a knoll above the lake, hidden from the view of fishermen below. As I began to climb the stairs, a humming sound increased as if the tower were singing to me. There was no shimmy to the tower, no movement, making the sound a bit startling. I was unable to discover what caused the hum.

Built in 1984, the eighty foot tower replaced an older 1930's era structure. The stairs, made of expanded metal, are unusual as the risers are set twelve inches apart, making it a bit of a stretch for short legs. The cat walk around the seven-foot square cab is also made of expanded metal, giving the look out a view of the ground eighty feet below. If visitors forgets to look off at the horizon or fails to focus on the metal floor, the view can be a bit startling between their feet. Solar panels extending from the tower provide power for the lookout.

The northern border of the San Carlos is the Fort Apache Reservation. The lookout at Maverick on Fort Apache tells me that he frequently picks up the reports from Dry Lake, triangulating their sightings. The lookouts seem able to determine which reservation holds a fire, which is impressive considering there are no boundary lines painted across the tree tops. It pays to know the nuances of the terrain.

Point of Pines, located northwest of the tower, is a substation for the San Carlos Forestry department. Recreation seems to be a very important part of the tourism dollars that come to the reservation and so the tower serves an important role in protecting this beautiful area.

San Carlos Apache Reservation

Hilltop / San Carlos Apache Reservation

Tower: Hilltop
Year Built: 1930
Height: 3'
Manufacture: San Carlos Tribe
Model: Wood Cabin
Elevation: 6,628'
Access: Road
Rating: Active

Hilltop is one of two fire towers in Arizona that sits on the transition between the pinyon-juniper zone and the high grasslands. It is a desert tower, or in this case, a cabin. Built by the San Carlos tribe in the 1930's, the wood frame cabin is a bit different from the standard L4 and L5 models. The front and one side of the cabin have a covered porch with steps rising from the ground three feet below. The porches give the impression that this is a great place to watch the sunrise. The cabin sits on wood risers lifting it above ground level which probably is good in snake territory. The windows date from an early era with multiple panes set in wood frames. The roof line also varies from the standard models.

Driving up to the cabin, I was struck by the desolation of the rocky hillsides, a sparse population of juniper and pinyon clinging to the thin soil. Studying the example set by the Cave Creek Complex fire near Phoenix, there is little doubt that a fire could roar through the sparse forest but after the drive across the desert landscape, one wonders about the need for a lookout. It is very isolated territory, a bare hilltop accessed by a long dusty road.

Yet I found myself soaking in the views, turning round and round to catch each canyon and ridge. Far in the distance is San Carlos. At least I knew it was there after the long drive but I could not see the outline of the small community through the dusty haze.

A small trailer near the cabin offers a home to the lookout should he choose to stay overnight rather than make the long commute each morning and evening. A chain link fence surrounds the compound, protecting the facility from vandalism. Visitors are usually employees of the Apache Forestry Department. White visitors rarely find their way to this isolated corner of the reservation.

The tower stands watch over the western end of the San Carlos. It is not far from the site of Dads Lookout which was dismantled a number of years ago. Despite the unusual name, there seems to be little information on Dads Lookout.

Hilltop

San Carlos Apache Reservation

Extinct

Edwards
Year Built: 1938
Height: 54'
Manufacture: Aermotor
Model: 7 x 7 cab
Elevation: 6,404'
Reservation: San Carlos Apache

Old Summit
Year Built: 1969
Height: 54'
Manufacture: Aermotor ?
Model: 7 x 7 cab
Elevation: 7,470'
Reservation: San Carlos Apache

Willow Mountain
Year Built: 1930
Height: 20'
Manufacture: San Carlos IR
Model: Wood Cabin
Elevation: 7,817'
Reservation: San Carlos

Dads Lookout
Height: 3'
Manufacture: San Carlos IR
Model: Wood Cabin
Reservation: Fort Apache
Cabin was located north of Hilltop. No information on origin of name.

The Geronimo Hot Shots

Fifteen years ago, the San Carlos Reservation was home only to Type Two fire crews. Wilber Balvado set out to change that, giving the reservation its own Type One Hot Shot crew. They trained their crews, setting up a chain of command with a supervisor, an assistant, a foreman and three squad bosses - all pretty standard for the Type One crews. For a year they trained, practiced and were observed before becoming a designated hot shot crew. They are named for a small town on the reservation. A crew cannot be named for a specific individual. It still seems somewhat suitable that the modern day warriors of the Apache Tribe carry the same name as one of their notable chiefs. But that is only the beginning of the story.

Today the Geronimo Hot Shots are considered among the best in the country. They gathered one warm afternoon at the end of their season in a small block building on the grounds of the San Carlos Apache Reservation Forestry Headquarters. They were burned out. There is no other way to put it. They had been gone all season on sixteen large fires and that didn't begin to count the seven hundred fires San Carlos Forestry crews, Type 1 and Type 2, had responded to on their own reservation since April. Many of the fires had been grass fires, many human caused.

The Geronimo Hot Shots had begun their season seven months earlier after a three month hiatus, ready to get back to work. They started with training, running and doing drills. When the time came to choose the crew the men had to run one and a half miles in ten minutes, a fairly easy task for most of them. They had to do twenty five pushups in one minute, forty sit ups in one minute and a number of pull ups based on their weight. They submitted to drug tests, staying clean, knowing it would matter when the flames rose against them. As the season progressed they knew they would depend on each other, calling their team mates their family for the next eight to nine months.

The job pays fairly well for the reservation and young men are eager to attain the status of Apache Hot Shot, not just for the money but for the pride of doing the job well. They earn about $25 to $30 thousand dollars over the nine month season. While the most intense period fighting wild-

The Geronimo Hot Shots

San Carlos Apache Reservation

179

fires lasts through the hot months of summer, the last two months of the fire season are usually spent doing clean up work on Reservation land. This is considered a good paying job by reservation standards. And they earn it.

Photo: Dave Lorentz

They race through the summer, constantly traveling to fires throughout the west. They may come home for two days and complain that they race around, trying to catch up on all their chores before they are called out again. Somehow it doesn't seem like a day off. They shake their heads and say they have no life. "It's a tough job, if you can handle it."

When I asked what the worse part of the job was, one said they hardly ever get a shower out in the field. Another said being away from family. They all agreed with that. They mentioned that many of the fires are in areas with no cell phone service - they can't call home. And they know little of what is going on in the world when they are out on a fire.

Then, they recalled Sept. 11, 2001. They had just reached a fire up north in Montana and the crews gathered around their foreman to hear their orders. Instead, he called them around a radio and they heard that a plane had hit the Twin Towers. It didn't really sink in even as they were told there would be no fire fight that day and they could return to their camp. Even when they learned that the helicopters were grounded and would not fight the fire with them, they remained in a private world where the danger is defined by one hundred foot flames. In time they gathered around a small TV and learned for the first time of the devastation wreaked on New York. Sitting at headquarters four years later, they fell silent as they recalled that moment shared with the rest of the world.

I was surprised that they feel such an affinity for the world outside their reservation borders. They have traveled to many neighboring states, even Alaska. It gives them a world view. A couple of the men had come to the crew out of high school. Some had spent a couple of seasons on a type two crew before moving up to the Hot Shots. This is true of Wilber Balvado's two sons.

They leave the Reservation for most fire lines in 'crew buggies'. These are square trucks with a cab on the front for two drivers. Eight men sit in the back, with no air conditioning, no heat. They freeze, they broil. They go to a new fire. Those who can sleep in a cramped sitting position do the best on their long commute between fires. When they reach the staging site they tumble out of the crew buggy as their superintendent goes off to check with the incident commander. He is usually sent to a planning meeting. He then briefs the crew, telling them where they will go and what is expected on each fire. He describes weather conditions and the precautions they must keep in mind even as they pull on their fire resistant yellow shirts and dark green pants over calf high boots. They shoulder bags that weigh forty, fifty, even sixty pounds with equipment and as much as seven quarts of water. The foreman scouts the fire line, working ahead of the crew, setting their route and seeking escape routes. He also sets one man with radio communication as a lookout at a distant location in case the fire flares up, threatening to trap the crew.

Behind the foreman come the sawyers, wielding chain saws with twenty eight inch blades. Almost all of the crew is certified to wield a chain saw but those who hold that position in the line are proud of their work. They describe a feeling of exhilaration as they begin to work on a tree, setting their cuts and pulling the crew back as it falls. An 'A' faller is certified to fell trees about four inches in diameter, a 'B' faller will take out trees the size of light posts but a 'C' faller is given the more difficult trees either due to their size, a strange formation or if the tree is already burning. Even after moving on to another position, a sawyer yearns just a bit to once again wield a saw. They will tell you that each has his own saw, his baby. He knows the idiosyncracies of that saw. He is reluctant to allow any one else to touch it, to use it just as he is reluctant to use another saw.

Behind the sawyers come the men with pulaskis, chopping at the dirt, pulling up roots, pushing aside boulders, creating a virtual highway of a fire line through timber. Finally the men with rhinos follow the pulaskis, dousing smoking snags and burning embers.

As they cut a fire line, they take pride in "bumping" other crews. They are initially given a section of line to cut, working quickly to catch the crew in front of them, only to leap frog beyond that crew to a new section of line until they are out in front leading the charge against the fire.

At headquarters, I asked Wilber if he hears about the close calls. Not only has he helped to form the Hot Shots, but his sons now work the line. He nods and agrees that sometimes he becomes a little tense when he hears about a close call to his crews, like the one in Montana in 2004.

The crew had been assigned to cut a line on a north facing slope where the timber was dense. The previous day the fire had been spotting ahead of the line of flame, throwing embers ahead that began smoking in the thick brush. The Geronimo Hots Shots were the only crew assigned to clean up the slope and worked steadily throughout the morning. Their lookout was assigned to watch from a hillside across from the work site. About one o'clock, as afternoon temperature began to climb, the fire blew up, its intensity increasing. The fire began to run and the lookout called the crews off the line. Two crews took off up hill while a third crew working toward the base of the slope ran straight downhill, trying to work around the fire. Running up hill is tough, and looking back, the guys laughed about one rookie. He quickly tired of the rapid pace and came to a stop. The men were only forty feet ahead of a hundred foot wall of flames. They screamed at the rookie, "Do you want to die or do you want to go home?" Somehow, with the flames closing in, he failed to realize their dire situation. They ripped him out of his complacency, forcing him up hill, ahead of the flames. When they reached their vehicles, they drove around the fire site, to pick up the remainder of the crew near the base of the hill as they struggled away from the fire.

The crew member, who was the lookout, shook his head at me. "I could see them working, the flames coming down on them as I called in a report. Then all I could do was wait. The smoke hid what was happening. I had to wait and see if they would come out." It was a terrible moment as he waited to see if 'his family', the men he worked with each day, would survive a close call.

The crew starts with twenty two members. By the time the active fire season begins to slow down their number has fallen to around fourteen members. Injuries have taken their toll. Sprained ankles, injured backs, infected feet remove men from the line. But there are moments of satisfaction when they close out a fire. Or when they show up at a staging area, striding toward the fire line, equipment hefted over their shoulders, a cheer goes up from the other fire crews. "All right, we got it now! The Apaches are here!"

It is a young man's job. Their ages range from twenty to twenty eight. Only three are married. They all know that a time will come when they will turn to other means of support and leave the life to someone younger. But for the moment, it is their job, their pride in a job well done.

Above: The old Humboldt Fire Tower. Below: The new Humboldt Fire Tower. Each representing two different eras in the history of Arizona's fire towers. The new tower is dwarfed by the massive Doppler Radar Dome.

The Tonto National Forest

Chapter 10

The Tonto National Forest is the fifth largest in the United States, covering almost three million acres. Elevations sink as low as 1,300 feet and rise to 7,900 feet. Due to its close proximity to some of our metropolitan areas, some parts of the Tonto are known as urban forest, an oxymoron in the language of the caretakers of our remaining wilderness. Those precious pockets of surviving open space that interface with our urban areas have become incredibly important to the population of Phoenix. On weekends, urban residents escape from their homes and offices to seek a little time reconnecting with the natural environment represented in these remaining pockets of wilderness.

The Tonto Forest is divided into six districts. It is bordered on the south by the cities of Mesa and Apache Junction, to the north by the Mogollon Rim. Two Apache Reservations form the eastern border.

Tonto National Forest

The Tonto is dissected by two of our major rivers, the Salt and the Verde with riparian areas that are unique in our dry climate. The Forest is also the watershed for six major reservoirs that store water for the Phoenix metropolitan area as well as what remains of agriculture in our rapidly growing state. Grazing is also an important consideration on the Tonto and is carefully managed as the dry terrain may be slow to recover from poor management practices. Eight wilderness areas exist within the Tonto, covering 600,000 acres.

The fire season is most active from May to mid July though this is a bit deceptive in a region that has seen a decade of drought under intense summer heat. On the Tonto, wild fire is a year-round consideration, averaging 330 wildfires per year for the last ten years. They are caused by both man and the lightning that comes from seasonal thunderstorms. The lookout at Humboldt describes his position as the lightening zone and notes that desert thunderstorms are spectacular.

The Forest has seven towers with two additional sites, now defunct. While we associate fire towers with forests, the Tonto has a unique 'desert tower' at Humboldt, surrounded by mesquite and manzanita. It is one of the few towers in the state with air conditioning.

Aztec / Tonto National Forest

Aztec Fire Tower was one of the earliest sites for observation on the Tonto National Forest. From the peak it is possible to see Roosevelt Lake to the west and into the San Carlos Apache Reservation on the east. At its base are the Sierra Anchas with thick forests and rugged terrain that is very tough for seasoned fire fighters.

A cabin was first built at the summit in 1925 and replaced in 1957 with a forty-one foot tower. The original structure was a D-6 cupola model

Tower: Aztec	Model: R-6 flat
Year Built: 1957	Elevation: 7,694'
Height: 41.3'	District: Pleasant Valley
Manufacture: International Derrick	Access: Road Rating: Active

The original Atec cupola-style cabin built in 1925.
Photo: Tonto N.F. Archives

Aztec

which consisted of a cabin with an observation deck surrounded by windows built above the living space. There are no cupola-style cabins remaining in Arizona under the US Forest Service. They have been replaced by towers that offer better observation. Due to the long, rough access lookouts use the twelve by twelve foot cab on Aztec as a live-in facility.

The road to Aztec follows Workman Creek, crossing at the top of the one of the most spectacular spring-time waterfalls in Arizona. The creek has not been kind to the lookouts that work Aztec as it has undermined the road till access has become somewhat precarious.

Aztec was the last tower for lookout Edward Abby as he wrote about the southwest, both in fiction and non-fictional genre. Toward the end of his days as a lookout, there was some suggestion that he spent more time staring at the typewriter than the horizon. He in turn, tongue-in-cheek, mocked his critics in his writing. Today, the Forest Service while aware that its lookouts may pursue personal hobbies, insists such activities must not distract their attention from the forest below. Each lookout develops his own routine to keep mentally alert, some pursuing limited activities while others pace the cab, binoculars in hand, ready to check the slightest trace of smoke.

Tonto National Forest

Colcord / Tonto National Forest

Tower: Colcord
Year Built: 1960
Height: 83'
Manufacture:
  USDA Forest Service
  CL 100-106

Model: R-6 flat. 12 x 12' cab
  with catwalk
Elevation: 7,513'
District: Pleasant Valley / Tonto
Access: Road
Rating: Active

Colcord Fire Tower stands on a knobby peak overlooking State Route 260, east of Payson. It is one of a chain of towers between Payson and Springerville. While it is not considered by some in the district as a primary tower, it is essential for the safety of the small communities that line the highway. If a fire were to sweep through Colcord, Forest Service personnel acknowledge they would be hard pressed to evacuate all the small communities along SR260. Colcord plays a significant role in keeping watch over such a volatile area.

Along with the threat from the highway, with its steady hum of traffic, the area is very popular for recreation at a number of small lakes and campgrounds. The tower also stands watch over the upper reaches of the Sierra Anchas and into Pleasant Valley. The area has seen some significant fires in the past and crews work at thinning the forest to diminish the threat of fire.

A fifty-foot tower with an LX-24 cab was first built at the site in 1925. A second thirty-five tower, also with an LX-24 cab was built in 1928. The two towers stood within a short distance of each other. According to Forest Service personnel, both towers were worked at the same time, though no one seems to recall why this happened.. If the competition is stiff now to keep other lookouts from reporting a smoke rising from one's backyard, it must have been cut throat with two towers within shouting distance of each other. The current structure, built in 1960, is one of the taller towers in the region at 82 feet with a twelve by twelve foot live-in cab.

The current tower was notable at one time for a rainwater collection system with gutters funneling rainwater off the roof into a cistern below the tower. Many of the cisterns for the state's towers are currently unusable, cracked by age, their contents unable to pass state inspection standards. Instead water is hauled to each site by Forest Service personnel. Often the lookouts bring their own drinking water in plastic jugs. While the cistern does not supply all the demand from Colcord, it helps reduce the amount of water the Forest Service must haul to the site.

Colcord

Tonto National Forest

Diamond Point / Tonto National Forest

Diamond Point tower has stood east of Payson, on the north side of Route 260, since 1936 when it replaced an earlier tower built in 1925. The manufacturer, Pacific Coast Steel, supplied only four other towers to the Forest Service in Arizona. The cab at twelve by twelve feet is considered large enough to be lived in though the current lookout prefers to commute to work each day.

The tower has been well maintained with a catwalk added to the exterior of the cab in 2006. At the base of the tower, a small cabin was once used as a residence for the lookout. It is now used primarily for storage. A barn built in 1941 was destroyed by fire in 1972

In 2006, Dee was in her 18th season as a lookout though she has worked for the Forest Service for 26 years. Like many of the lookouts, she began on an engine crew, followed by duty with a trail crew before she took the

A catwalk was added to the tower in late 2006.

Tower: Diamond Point	Model: L-4, 12 x 12 cab
Year Built: 1936	Elevation: 6,384'
Height: 30'	District: Payson / Tonto
Manufacture: Pacific Coast Steel	Access: Road
	Rating: Active

position as lookout. In the previous season she had recorded thirty first sitings for her tower alone. She is highly respected by the crews who often ask her to relay requests to the dispatch center even when they might be within range of the repeater. She describes being a lookout as the perfect job except for the lack of benefits. It allows her to enjoy time camping and hiking in the wilderness that she helps protect from her tower.

Dee has always had dogs on the tower, the latest being a two year old heeler rottweiler mix named Blaze. The

Blaze, the canine lookout, on duty.
Photo: Mark Caswell

dog raced down the stairs to meet us as we approached and then eagerly returned to Dee to report who he had found. The day we visited he was a busy dog. We found the Highway Patrol engaged in a training exercise for their swat team on the peak. They had informed Dee well in advance that men with rifles would be roaming the peak under her observation.

Set on the Mogollon rim, Diamond Point is part of a chain of towers that stretch across the eastern half of Arizona on the Rim.

Diamond Point

Tonto National Forest

Humboldt / Tonto National Forest

Humboldt is one of the few towers in the state located exclusively in desert terrain and contains an air conditioner for the comfort of the lookout. When Thomas calls in his weather report each morning his temperature readings soar above other towers on the district. He wonders if they all laugh at him.

The interior of the fourteen-foot square cab was renovated in March

Tower: Humboldt
Year Built: 1958
Height: 30'
Manufacture:
    Civil Aeronautics Admin.

Model: R-6 flat
Elevation: 5,204'
District: Cave Creek / Tonto
Access: Road
Rating: Active

2006. The tower is listed on the Historical Register and the exterior cannot be changed. The tower stands watch over Horseshoe and Bartlett Lakes, the Matazals, Four Peaks and the region north to Payson. The tower sits in the lightening zone with ninety per cent of the fires caused by lightening.

The last two years Thomas has been burned out of the tower. In 2005, the Cave Creek fire broke out south of his tower at 4:30 in the afternoon followed by the Humboldt fire to the southeast at 6:00. The fires were burning under heavy transmission lines and the fire crews were limited in their efforts. Tom could not believe the speed at which each fire spread. Both fires jumped dirt roads that crews had hoped would serve as fire breaks. He knew it was time to leave as the fire came up the hill at him once again. He first called Dispatch, informing them that he had to evacuate. As he drove along the narrow track, through flames on both sides of the road, he pleaded "tires don't fail me now!"

As he left, the fire had trapped a fire crew on the hillside. They hunkered down to see what direction the fire would run before making a break for clear air. Tom returned to the tower within a couple of days of the fire sweeping over the peak as he could still stand watch over the areas that were not threatened by the flames.

The one lane road to the tower follows the contours of the low peak. The last stretch winds around the edge of the hill with only a guardrail between the narrow lane and a steep drop off. Some drivers wonder why they ever committed to the drive. They are committed. There is no turn around at this point.

Humboldt Fire Tower is dominated by a Doppler radar dome towering over the lookout. What would stand as a significant landmark on its own, is reduced to a secondary feature next to the massive dome that resembles a golf ball set on a giant tee. A constant hum emanates from the dome. The tie between the two structures is inescapable as one records meteorological readings while the other reports the wildfires sparked by lightening strikes. Tom says the structure of the dome has not prevented him from reporting the smoke that rise within his oversight.

Humboldt

Tonto National Forest

McFadden Peak / Tonto National Forest

This 1960's era, two-story cinder block based tower replaced a twenty foot Aermotor tower that had been built in 1927.

Tower: McFadden
Year Built: 1964
Height: 10'
Manufacture: USDA Forest Service CL 100-106
Model: R-6 flat, 14 x 14' cab with catwalk
Elevation: 7,135'
District: Pleasant Valley / Tonto
Access: Road
Rating: Active

McFadden Peak

McFadden Peak is centrally located along the spine of the Sierra Anchas. The McFadden tower covers the middle ground between Colcord tower to the north and Aztec tower to the south, giving full coverage to the rocky peaks and steep valleys of this rugged range.

A twenty-foot Aermotor tower was first built at the site in 1927. This was replaced by a ten-foot tower in 1964. The base is built of cinder block while the upper level is a fourteen-foot square steel cab with windows offering a 360 degree view. Denzil, the lookout, has been with the forest service since the mid 1960's when he reputedly worked as a helijumper. These men and women jump without repelling by rope as the helicopters hover just above the ground. It is a rough profession, prone to injury.

Denzil is a quiet individual, hard to coax into saying more than two words at a time when he opens his mouth to speak. After thirty years, he may currently be the most experienced lookout in Arizona. He is cordial to visitors and if they take a moment, they may realize from the stack of magazines resting on one bunk that Denzil has a wide variety of interests. His photography, featured on greeting cards, has been sold at the Ranger Station in Young.

The little town of Young is situated in what was known as Pleasant Valley, at the base of McFadden Peak. It is the site of the feud between the Grahams and the Tewksburys back in the 1800s. Today, about 800 to 1000 people live in the area, depending on the season. The Forest Service, along with state and county government, are the largest employers. Tourism also brings visitors into the valley along state route 288, one of three dirt roads designated as official highways in Arizona.

The tower stands watch over the highway and the flow of traffic that may bring harm to the region's forest. Lightning is also a large contributor to wildfire. The high points have some spectacular views over the range and across Roosevelt Lake. The catwalk of the tower allows visitors to check out the view without working too hard, providing they can handle the drive along a narrow dirt track, with no guard rail, up to the tower.

Tonto National Forest

Mount Ord / Tonto National Forest

In the 1980's, the communications companies proposed placing towers at the summit of Mount Ord. The Forest Service protested that their towers would block the view of the fifty-nine foot fire tower that had stood since 1936. The communication companies agreed to replace the old tower with a new hundred foot structure topped by a fourteen-foot square cab. The old MC-39 Aermotor tower was moved to South Mountain Park in Phoenix as part of an educational display.

The original cabin built in 1935 still stands below the tower in a

Tower: Mount Ord	Model: R-6 flat
Year Built: 1983	Elevation: 7128'
Height: 102'	District: Mesa / Tonto
Manufacture:	Access: Road
USDA Forest Service CL 100-106	Rating: Active

grove of oak trees. A wide covered porch fronts the cabin. Inside, wood cabinets, a double bed, a wood stove, a couch and modern appliances make a comfortable home for the lookouts. A shower shack crowds the edge of the cabin's porch with a storage building off to one side. The shower is filled with sediment and no longer used.

The tower also has a bunk and appliances in the cab should the lookout choose to stay a hundred feet above ground. The lookout noted that when the winds rise at night, the tower begins to rock, something like a cradle. The tower has a hand operated winch that allows the lookout to haul supplies up to the cab without carrying them up the stairs. Gutters set along the flat roof collect rainwater for the lookout.

Modern windows forty-eight inches above the floor allow the lookout to stand watch over the lakes along the Salt River as well as the Mazatals, the Sierra Anchas, Four Peaks and the Superstitions. The lookout has a view of the Mogollon Rim to the north and SR 87 as its winds over the rim to Payson. The traffic along SR87 may be one of the biggest contributors to wildfire along with the lightning strikes from summer storms. The lookout describes the lightning storms as spectacular, the clouds building to the east to spread across the peaks below his tower.

Dust devils kick up across earlier burns. The lookout compared their image to smoke rising above the hills below. He watches them before making a call. He would hate to report a dust devil, conscious of the cost of chasing a smoke. But then he wonders, what if it was smoke? Second guessing can become an occupational hazard.

Mount Ord, due to its close proximity to an urban area, receives a number of visitors each season. It is popular with the Boy Scouts who come to learn more about the role of the lookout. Most storm up the steps and along the balcony. A few inch along, their backs pressed against the wall into the cabin. The lookout often hears them talking about the fear factor in climbing the tower. He laughs about the women who fearlessly climb the tower, leaving their husbands on the ground below, offering distant support.

Mount Ord

Tonto National Forest

Signal Peak / Tonto National Forest

Photo: Mark Caswell

Tower: Signal Peak
Year Built: 1934
Height: 59.3'
Manufacture: Aermotor MC-39
Model: 7 x 7 cab

Elevation: 7812'
District: Globe / Tonto
Access: Road
Rating: Active

Signal Peak

Silver first brought settlers to the Pinal Mountains. The rich veins of copper helped found the city of Globe. Signal Peak is the highest point in the Pinals, overlooking the mining towns of Globe, Miami and Superior. The hillsides below the tower have a number of mining shafts and natural caves, remnants of man's history in the Pinal Mountains.

In the 1920's, the Forest Service built a fire tower on Signal Peak to stand watch over the mountain range and the small mining communities at their base. In 1934, the CCC replaced the original 1920's era tower with an Aermotor MC-39, topped by the standard seven foot square cab.

Fifty years later the 1930's era tower was declared unsafe. The lookout sat in his car watching the surrounding peaks. Observation was very limited. The Forest Service hired a contractor in the mid 1980's to make sufficient repairs so that the lookout could once again use the tower. The tower will be replaced when tight budgets allow though the Forest Supervisor is uncertain about when that will happen. Plans call for a fourteen foot square cab set on a fifty-foot tower.

Just below the peak, a number of private cabins offer refuge from the heat of the desert among the tall pines. When fire raced up the hillside, these cabins became natural prey, flaming against the dark sky as each in turn went up in flames. A side canyon acted as a chimney, funneling hot vapors and flames up the side of the peak in just thirty minutes. Residents of Globe watched in horror, cheering on the fire crews, mourning the damage to their recreational area. A few cabins survived the onslaught. The area is now recovering with lush green vegetation crowding the burned totems.

At the base of the tower, a historic cabin offers quarters for the lookout. The cabin was built in 1935 with two rooms added in 1985. A barn once stood on the site but has been removed.

Tonto National Forest

Former Towers / Tonto National Forest

Ferndell
Year Built: 1930's
Height: 3'
Manufacture: Forest Service
Model: Wood Cabin
Elevation: 7,750'
District: Globe

Madera Peak
Year Built: possibly 1930's
Height: 40'
Manufacture: Aermotor base
Model: wood cabin
Elevation: 6,647'
District: Globe

Madera Peak Fire Tower
Photo: Tonto NF Archives

The Prescott National Forest

Chapter 11

The Prescott National Forest is divided by state land into two halves, east and west. It covers 1.25 million acres with elevations ranging from 3,000 to 8,000 feet. The eastern half includes the Black Hills, Mingus Mountain, Black Mesa, part of the Sycamore Wilderness area and the headwaters of the Verde River. The western half extends over the Juniper, Santa Maria, Sierra Prieta and Bradshaw Mountains. Prescott, with the Supervisors Office, is centrally located between the eastern and western halves of the Forest.

The Prescott National Forest has become a playground for many residents of the Phoenix metropolitan area, creating a challenge for forest personnel who attempt to maintain the pristine wilderness experience. Six towers stand watch over this Forest. One other location has been identified as the site of a fire tower, now removed. Of the six towers, Hyde Mountain is no longer active.

When seeking information, it is helpful to understand that the Prescott National Forest is broken into three districts. The Bradshaw district, south of Prescott, includes

Tony Nelson,

Horsethief Lookout

the Bradshaw Mountains and the Granite Wilderness area with Mount Union as the highest point. The Chino Valley district, north of Prescott, includes the Juniper Mesa, Apache Creek and Woodchute wilderness areas as well as the popular recreation area at Camp Wood. The Verde district stretches along the Verde River and along parts of Oak Creek Canyon.

The history of the region stretches back to the earliest settlement in our state. History buffs could spend a lifetime learning about the different cultures that lived in what would become the Prescott National Forest

Horse Thief / Prescott National Forest

Tony Nelson proudly explains that Horsethief tower is a family project. His great uncle constructed the tower in 1934. His uncle was the first lookout and now Tony stands watch, reporting thirty-nine first strikes in 2005. He notes that the area has a history for big fires and takes his job seriously with the hope of preventing the next big one. When the Cave Creek complex fires broke out

Tower: Horsethief
Year Built: 1934
Height: 40'
Manufacture:
　Pacific Steel Co.
Model: L-4 or D-2
Elevation: 6,704'
District:
　Bradshaw / Prescott
Access: Road
Rating: Active

The tower has been heavily modified with new windows in 1976 & 1983, a new roof in 1983 and siding in 1984.

Horse Thief

in May 2005, Tony had a front row seat with the flames gleaming red at night, smoke billowing up during the warm afternoons.

He describes a direct strike to his tower as a big 'ker--pow' with lightening branching down the sides like the roots of a tree. But his most spectacular memory was a strike in the 1950's. A telephone wire ran from the Horse Thief tower over to Crown King dispatch and up to Towers Lookout. When lightening struck the tower, it arced along the telephone line to the fire finder in the center of the cab. Flames illuminated the cab of the tower. Tony stood wide-eyed mere feet from the flames. He had just graduated from high school. He spent that memorable summer reporting lightening strikes before he went to work in the mines around Crown King. Years later, after retiring from the construction trade, he returned to Horse Thief tower. The cab shows his handiwork as he has refinished the inside in hardwood paneling.

From the tower he scans the terrain from Bill Williams Mountain west of Flagstaff, down I-17 to the Mazatals and south to Phoenix. His panoramic view of Lake Pleasant by day and the lights of Phoenix at night is spectacular. He watches the southeastern side of the Bradshaws, all visible from just three flights above ground level. From the peak, the terrain below his tower drops 5000 feet into Bloody Basin.

He noted that an experienced fire lookout gains an intimacy with the topography of his region so that he immediately spots something out of place with just the naked eye. I had noticed this with other lookouts. While simply scanning the horizon, they would reach for the binoculars, checking a location that looked like any other mountainside to me.

This is the history of someone who grew up in the mountains, who has hunted and hiked the forest for years, making it his own. Tony is the oldest surviving native of Crown King and recalls that growing up in the community, he didn't get away with anything. Today, the community has changed with a number of vacation homes rising through the rock outcroppings and pines of the community, tucked away at the peak of the Bradshaws.

Prescott National Forest

Hyde Mountain / Prescott National Forest

The Hyde Mountain Fire cabin is no longer actively used for observation by the Forest Service but it remains on the list of lookouts for the Prescott National Forest. The ten-foot square L-5 cabin sits on a peak overlooking the Santa Maria Mountains, the Juniper Mesa and Apache Creek Wilderness areas as well as portions of the Williamson Valley. There is no road to the cabin. Visitors drive to Camp Wood, the site of a former CCC camp, to access the trail to the cabin. The trail is a two mile hike that follows the

Tower: Hyde Mountain
Year Built: 1936
Height: 3'
Manufacture: Forest Service
Model: L-5, 10 x 10' cabin
Elevation: 7,272'
District: Chino Valley / Prescott
Access: Trail
Rating: Inactive

contours of Hyde Peak, rising above the ponderosa pine forest for an excellent view of the surrounding country. Visitors can see north to the San Francisco Peaks and Bill Williams Mountain, south to Granite Mountain and the Bradshaws.

The 1930's era cabin is usually shuttered though it may be possible to lift the heavy panel for a glimpse inside. The bunk and fire finder have been removed but the kitchen counter remains along with a chair. Near the cabin, sits a rack of solar panels that power two communication antennas behind the cabin. It is an interesting contrast: the depression era cabin with modern communication equipment. A small outhouse sits below the peak, down a narrow brush shrouded path. As the lookout sits within the wilderness boundary, access is limited to foot or bicycle.

A private research group rents the cabin sporadi-

Hyde Mtn

cally for a fee to the Forest Service. The Camp Wood site at the base of the peak is popular with outdoor enthusiasts and frequently hosts hunters' camps. A recent fire west of Camp Wood has left powdery ash and blackened brush under the forest canopy along the road to the lookout. It is a good reminder of the role of a fire lookout though the fire was sited from another tower.

Prescott National Forest

Mingus Mountain / Prescott National Forest

Tower: Mingus Mountain
Year Built: 1935
Height: 59.3'
Manufacture:
   Pacific Coast Steel

Model: 7 x 7 cab
Elevation: 7,743'
District: Bradshaw / Prescott
Access: Road
Rating: Active

Mingus Mountain

Prescott National Forest

Jim Horn loves the moment when the campers gather on the parade ground at the church camp below his peak and the leaders tell the children "we are not alone. Lookout Jim is watching over us". They instruct the campers to turn and look at the Mingus Mountain tower. As the campers turn to look, Jim leans out with a friendly wave. They all respond with enthusiastic salutes. He recalls that quiet connection with a big smile in the solitude of his little cab elevated sixty feet in thin air.

The Mingus Mountain tower was built in the 1930's along with two small cabins at its base. One was used for housing while the second is a 'ten man cache' for fire crews. It is the lone tower on Mingus Mountain, overlooking the popular recreation areas as well as the Verde Valley. Despite the number of outdoor enthusiasts and the popular scenic route over Mingus Mountain between Prescott and the Verde Valley, few people find their way to the tower. Of those who do drive to the base, many stare up at the six flights of exposed stairs and decide not to climb the tower. Jim is more likely to be visited by hummingbirds who excel in aerial combat around his feeders. As a retired Air Force Colonel, he can appreciate the tactics of the little kamikazes. But his favorite bird siting was watching a mother hawk teaching her young to hunt pigeons one day outside the windows of his tower. She would soar high to dive on her prey, the young birds swooping after her, imitating each move.

Due to the drought that has afflicted northern Arizona for a number of years, Jim often spends ten hours a day six days a week in the little cab. He uses free weights and his cell phone to stay alert. He says that "if you go with the flow, looking for fire comes naturally."

When the winds began to rise, he talked about fighting the gusts along the stairway. In our ascent the winds were only 25 miles per hour. Yet I gripped the iron railing with white knuckles. When the winds reach 55 miles per hour, Jim may choose to ride the shuttering metal rather than descend through the wind tunnel created by the exposed stairway. As I descend, I feel the tower swaying and long for the safety of the ground. In high winds, it might be a tough choice.

Mount Union / Prescott National Forest

Mount Union is the highest point in the Yavapai County. The peak rises out of the Bradshaw Mountains about four miles, as the crow flies, south of Walker, a small community near Prescott. At the summit, a 1930's era fire tower surveys the eastern side of the Bradshaws. Several communication towers also sprout from the peak above a sea of trees. From the cab, the lookout can see Mount Union's sister tower on Spruce Peak, overlooking the north end of the Bradshaws. At the base of the thirty foot tower, stands a small cement block cabin housing some of the radio equipment.

Mount Union

Mount Union was named by the Walker Party when it explored the region in the 1800's. The Walker party included men loyal to the Confederate cause and men who owed their allegiance to the Union. Despite conflicting allegiance, the two groups got along quite well. When they came to two neighboring peaks in the Bradshaws the decision was made to name one Mt. Davis after the President of the Confederacy and the other Mount Union to honor the northern states who fought to keep our country united, free from secession.

A one bedroom cabin below the peak serves as home to the lookout. The original cabin burned down after a criminal suspect broke into the cabin one winter and took refuge from the law enforcement officials seeking him. The current lookout notes that the cabin is at 8,000 feet and in the morning he may wake up to find clouds floating through the cabin after leaving the windows open during the night.

He doesn't see much traffic as a gate was constructed across the road several years ago. Fire crews drop in for a visit. He describes them as rough, burly men with heavy packs who are some of the nicest guys he has ever known. When the fire season slows down, they may call him and beg, "John, find us a fire." Fire is what they do.

Several miles past the turnoff to Mount Union, along the Senator Highway, is an old stage coach stop that has been restored by the Forest Service. The 1930's era fire tower, a stage coach stop and the ruins of a stamp mill from the 1800's are all reminders of the active history of the Bradshaws over the past century.

Tower: Mount Union
Year Built: 1933, original cabin 1935
Height: 30'
Manufacture: Aermotor MC-24
Model: L-4, 12 x 12 cabin
Elevation: 7,978'
District: Bradshaw / Prescott
Access: Road
Rating: Active

Prescott National Forest

Spruce Mountain / Prescott National Forest

Tower: Spruce Mountain
Year Built: 1936
Height: 30'
Manufacture: Aermotor MC-24

Model: L-4, 12 x 12 cab
Elevation: 7,693'
District: Bradshaw / Prescott
Access: Road
Rating: Active

Spruce Mountain

Prescott National Forest

In the late 1900's, the population of Prescott and its neighboring communities exploded. Houses filled the valleys and ridges around Prescott. In 2004, fire swept along the ridges toward the community, forcing hundreds to evacuate. With the population growth, Spruce Mountain Lookout has attained a new urgency in the fight to preserve Prescott.

Spruce Mountain was built in 1936 on a rock knob overlooking Prescott, Prescott Valley and the western side of the Bradshaws. A short path leads up to the lookout from a parking area and ascends three flights to an entrance in the cabin floor. As I stood looking out over the territory, low lying clouds crept through the valleys below bringing to mind the hollows of the Appalachians. However, the bright gleam of desert plains beyond the edge of the Bradshaws brought me back mentally to Arizona, with a drought unrelieved by one winter of heavy snow. A trap door in the ceiling of the peaked roof of the tower was a reminder that there may not be adequate time to reach safety if a fire should sweep over the peak. The access is miles of dirt road off the Senator Highway. If flames threatened the tower, a helicopter could drop down on the tower and pick up the lookout from the roof.

In 2005, the lookout seems unperturbed by the threat, as she studied for an environmental degree. She told me her favorite moments are the lightening storms with fiery streaks dancing across the peaks. She waits them out in her glass insulated chair, watching the fireworks. When her kayaking partner arrived, he revealed that her laid back approach belied a fierce competitive streak that surfaces in a tight kayaking race. She simply smiled and showed me a chart on the wall. When she took over the duties for this tower, she promised the former lookout that she would maintain the tradition of painting rattlesnakes. There are three snakes that favor the granite rock formations around the tower. She pointed out the snake stick, the paint brush and the chart which showed the location on each snake to be painted for identification. As I climbed through dense brush around the formations, photographing the tower, I kept looking for a bright splotch of paint, hoping that all the 'painted sticks' were in their dens as rain drops began to fall.

Towers / Prescott National Forest

Towers Mountain may have been used as a lookout site as early as 1902, possibly with a lookout tree, predating many of the earliest observation sites in Arizona. In 1928, a one-room cabin was constructed for the lookouts. This was still in use in the mid 1980's when Bev Everson served as lookout. She

Tower: Tower Mountain
Year Built: 1933
Height: 30'
Manufacture: Pacific Coast Steel

Model: D-2, 12 x 12 cab
Elevation: 7,628'
District: Bradshaw / Prescott
Access: Road
Rating: Active

distinctly remembers sharing the cabin with spiders, centipedes and mice. The spiders frequently ran across the faces of Bev and her husband as they tried to sleep. "At night, it could sound like a three piece band when the mice invaded the drawer beneath the oven," she says.

The solar shower, consisting of three partial walls, was located outside, around the back of the cabin. She describes it as cold and windy. One night her husband hurried toward the shower only to notice the cabin wall pulsating when lit by his flashlight. Further inspection revealed that the wall was covered by daddy long-leg spiders, gymnastically flexing their legs in the light.

The couple was one of several lookouts to report that the old cabin was haunted. They recall heavy footsteps across the steeply pitched roof without a trace of tracks the next morning. Other lookouts reported voices or the jangle of harness and bugles sounding in the clear air. At night a chain of wavering lights could be seen moving across a distant hillside. Skeptics suggested the lights were mountain bikers out for a late ride. The tower was built on the site of an old Cavalry route and thus the basis for speculation about it being haunted by the Cavalry.

The old cabin has been moved to a location near the Crown King Market. It was replaced by a modern two room structure with a broad porch. The thirty-foot Pacific Coast Steel tower stands on a ridge above the cabin. It has an odd scaffolding on one side of the twelve foot square cab that Bev says was intended as a catwalk for the tower. The catwalk was never completed.

Bev also remembers an old dentist chair being hauled to the top of a cliff south of the tower where one lookout sat in the final moments of day light, surveying her territory as the sun set over the Bradshaws.

A number of communication towers have been built near the fire tower, giving the peak a crowded appearance. The tower is north of Crown King off the Senator Highway, a popular recreation area for cabin owners and weekend warriors.

Towers

Prescott National Forest

Former Towers / Prescott National Forest

Verde Valley / Jerome
Year Built: 1938
Height: 3'
Manufacture: Forest Service
Model: L-4, 12 x 12 foot cabin
Elevation: 3,880'
District: Verde

Aftermath of a fire, Webb Peak.

The Coronado National Forest

Chapter 12

The Coronado National Forest is spread over twelve widely dispersed mountain ranges in Arizona and New Mexico. The ranges are known as sky islands and support a diversity of animal and plant life that are not found at lower elevations. They survive because the mountain ranges perform as an island refuge, harboring the species at higher elevations. Elevation on the Coronado ranges from 3,000 feet to 10,720 feet on Mount Graham in the Pinolenos. The forest covers 1,780,000 acres.

The Coronado places a high priority on sustaining these unique sky islands and their fragile ecosystems. Incredibly, for such a large, diverse area only nine fire towers or cabins stand watch over the Forest. Four of the nine are used sporadically. This places a great deal of responsibility on the remaining five lookouts who frequently scan the ridge lines of distant peaks through the heat waves rising above an intervening desert plain. Seven other sites have been identified as once having towers that have been removed, either by natural forces or Forest Service work crews. The work of the lookouts is incredibly important as the Forest Service seeks to preserve the sky islands.

The Forest is split into five districts over the twelve mountain ranges, each separated from the others by private and state owned land. Moving clockwise, the Safford District in the northeastern corner includes the Pinolenos with Mount Graham, the Galiluros and the Santa Teresa ranges. The Douglas district in the southeast corner covers the Chiricahua range along with the Dragoon and Peloncillo ranges. The Sierra Vista District, southcentral, includes the Huachuchas, the Patagonias and the Whetstone ranges. The Nogales district in the southwestern corner covers the Santa Ritas, the Pajaritos and Pajarita Wilderness area, the Tumacacories and the grasslands around Pena Blanca Lake. The Catalina district is centrally located over the Catalina Range and the Pusch Range wilderness, including the popular Sabino Canyon. The Catalina borders the Sahuaro National Monument. The Forest Supervisors Office in located in Tucson.

Coronado National Forest

Atascosa / Coronado National Forest

Tower: Atascosa
Year Built: 1933
Height: 3'
Manufacture: USDA Forest Service / CCC
Model: L-4 cabin
Elevation: 6,249'
District: Nogales / Coronado
Access: Trail
Rating: Inactive, currently hiker's rest house

Atascosa

Tucked away in a secluded corner of Arizona, overlooking the Mexican border, a little cabin tops Atascosa Peak. No longer used to house lookouts, Atascosa Peak is now used as a hikers rest house. Stepping inside, visitors find a couple of cots and shelves stocked with cooking equipment. There may be an extra supply of water for those who have run out on the ascent. A couple of camp chairs allow visitors to sit inside or out, contemplating the view.

On the table visitors may find a journal that offers a glimpse into the lives of the people who pass through the decommissioned lookout. The journal allows hikers an opportunity to pass on their comments or reveal a little of some passion in life. Each year, on December 31, a group hikes up from Nogales to the small cabin to celebrate the last moments of the old year, passing into the new. With each new year, they begin a new journal.

Atascosa Peak is the high point in the Atascosa Mountains that separate much of the Pajarita Wilderness from Pena Blanca Lake and the border community of Nogales. The mountains are covered with wild grasses and brush, with oak trees scattered across the gentle slopes. There is no road to the summit of Atascosa. A trail winds two and half miles up gentle grades along the contours of the peak to the summit. A ridge slopes away from the cabin, leaving it perched precariously on a rocky knob.

The cabin was built by the CCC under the auspices of the US Forest Service in 1933. In 1968, after 35 years of active use, archives record a request for cement anchors for the little building. It was declared unsafe without them and not suitable for occupation. Prior to this stern advice, how many lookouts wandered the wood floor, gazing through the windows, unaware that a strong gust might move them to a lower altitude? The Forest Service required 14,600 pounds of cement to anchor the cabin. It was recommended they use pre-mix cement delivered by helicoptor. Crews are still transported to the site by helicopter for maintenance even through the Forest Service has de-commissioned the cabin from official duty.

Coronado National Forest

Barfoot / Coronado National Forest

Tower: Barfoot
Year Built: 1935
Height: 3'
Manufacture: USDA Forest Service / CCC
Model: L-4 cabin, 12 x 12'
Elevation: 8,823'
District: Douglas / Coronado
Access: Trail
Rating: Inactive

Many visitors explore the Chiricahua National Monument but the more intrepid turn their vehicles up Pinery Canyon toward Onion Saddle and Rustler Park. It is a beautiful area with the park creating a little niche beneath a towering granite cliff. Overlooking Rustler Park is Barfoot Fire cabin.

Barfoot and Monte Vista are the two remaining lookouts from a series of towers that once stretched across the Chiricahua Mountains. When built, the cabin perched at the edge of a cliff, overlooking the Pinery Canyon Road, had sufficient oversight without the added height of a tower. The views over the northern end of the Chiricahuas remain wide open. The southern exposure is more contained by the encroaching forest. A rock wall below the cabin keeps visitors back from a sharp drop off. An outhouse and storage shed are also on site.

Barfoot Lookout, an L-4 ground level cabin, is the same design as the cabins at the summits of Sugar Loaf Mountain and Atascosa Peak. The three L-4 cabins were all part of the work done by the CCC in the 1930's, an era marked by great expansion for the Forest and Park Services. They are a glimpse into our history as we struggled to reconcile settlement with conservation in the wilderness that once covered the southwest. Today the cabin is seldom used, except in times of extreme fire danger.

At one time a fire tower stood on Fly Peak above Barfoot. It was removed due to vandalism though the cement anchors for the tower legs are still visible. To date, Barfoot has escaped the same fate.

There is no road to the lookout though FR 357 passes just below the peak. Lookouts assigned on a temporary basis hustle up the one mile trail to spend a few hours on duty. From the trail below the lookout, visitors looking east can get a glimpse of a crescent shaped burn that blackened the edge of the peak. The fire threatened Rustler Park and as flames approached the scenic recreational area, fire fighters desperately set a crescent-shaped back burn to stop the fire. The effort was successful and Rustler Park remains one of the hidden jewels in Arizona.

Barfoot

Coronado National Forest

Heliograph / Coronado National Forest

Tower: Heliograph
Year Built: 1933
Height: 100'
Manufacture: Aermotor MC-39
Model: 7 x 7 cab
Elevation: 10,022'
District: Safford / Coronado
Access: Road & Trail
Rating: Active

Heliograph

Coronado National Forest

In 2004, fire swept across the Pinolenos. Firefighters fought to save the Mount Graham telescope as well as the communications towers on nearby Heliograph Peak. But the moment came when they pulled back and flames attacked Heliograph fire tower. Only a helicopter could swoop down to drop slurry on the tower with the hope that the structure would survive. The flames ignited the wood floor of the cab and as it burned, the fire finder crashed eight stories to the ground below. The metal structure survived.

We found lookout Ron Arnold at the West Peak tower one year after Heliograph burned. He worked the West Peak tower as he waited to learn the fate of Heliograph from structural engineers.

It was a different assignment for him in that Heliograph had been a tower that frequently had visitors. Just a short distance off the Swift Trail, visitors could climb the eight flights of the hundred foot tower and learn about standing watch over the dense forests of the Pinolenos. West Peak is much more isolated than Heliograph and sees fewer visitors.

In 2006, engineers determined that the metal structure of the tower remained sound and that they could restore the tower to operation as it stood. The steps and base of the cab were replaced and a new fire finder was ordered. Only one company in the U.S. manufactures the Osbourne Fire Finder. The assistant FMO hopes to have the tower in operation in 2007.

On Heliograph Peak, visitors are subjected to a constant hum from the communication towers that have been restored to the summit. Two cabins remain, having been protected from the fire. One was for the lookout while the second served as a storage cache for fire crews. The tower overlooks the southern end of the Pinolenos. The view from the cab is simple awesome and worth climbing one hundred feet above ground level.

Heliograph Peak was named after the heliograph station set on its peak by the U.S. Cavalry in its battle against the Apaches as they tried to bring peace to the region. The Swift Trail, the campgrounds and possibly the tower were built by the CCC.

Lemmon Rock / Coronado National Forest

The Wildlife

As a congenial hermit, Stan leaves water bowls out for thirsty dogs, frisky chipmunks and black suited ravens. Human visitors would be well advised to sit at the front of the lookout as they discuss their family dramas rather than near the lookout door. Stan is more tolerant of the ravens who "abandon him on weekends to drop in on happy hour at the campgrounds." He may share his cabin with a ringtail but the chipmunks should stay outside. He has heard the scream of a mountain lion though they tend not to visit up close.

Tower: Lemmon Rock
Year Built: 1928
Height: 3'
Manufacture: Forest Service
Model: L-4 cabin
Elevation: 8,820'
District:
  Santa Catalina / Coronado
Access: Road & Trail
Rating: Active

Lemmon Rock

Walk into Lemmon Rock cabin and the panoramic view across the southern half of the Santa Catalinas leaves visitors speechless. Rocky canyons and pine shrouded peaks spread 180 degrees on either side. In the distance, Tucson shimmers in the desert sunlight

Standing watch at Lemmon Rock is quite possibly one of the strangest individuals I met in the research for this book. Stan genially tried to convince me that he was mildly deranged but I suspected the Forest Service would not have given him a radio if that was the case. Listening carefully to his verbal rambling and tales of urban legends, I began to hear the real work of a fire lookout creep forth He blends into the radio traffic as required, holding up a hand to take a call. In observing his panoramic view, I can see the responsibility and trust he has been given.

Lemmon Rock is a very popular spot on summer weekends, even though it is hidden below the peak and visitors must be willing to walk a bit to visit the little cabin. The lookout reports on average between 30 and 60 fires a season, as well as relaying traffic from units out of radio contact with headquarters. In an innovative move, Stan has added his own special touch with a digital camera and a computer by which he may send photos of smoke or a fire to dispatch

Stan has crammed every corner of the live-in cabin with the comforts of home, including a four burner stove, a full size refrigerator, a double sink, two bunks, coffee maker and an upholstered easy chair. He refers to his accommodations as the "Cadillac of the Catalinas." A flight of slate steps and a narrow walkway give access to the little cabin on its rocky knob.

When flames swept up the peak toward Summerhaven in the last devastating fire, the dispatcher warned Stan that he had fifteen minutes to get out. His ride was waiting at the top of the slope. They drove to the Palisades Ranger Station where he spent the next three weeks working in supply for the fire units battling the flames. By contrast, he has waded through two feet of snow to reach his post in early April. With no heat, the cabin can be icy those first couple of weeks but Stan returns each year for a new season.

Coronado National Forest

Monte Vista / Coronado National Forest

Tower: Monte Vista
Year Built: 1966
Height: 41.3'
Manufacture:
  USDA Forest Service
  CL 100-106

Model: R-6 flat, 14 x 14 cab
Elevation: 9,370
District: Douglas / Coronado
Access: Trail
Rating: Active

The man standing watch on Monte Vista came as close to a hermit of all the lookouts we met in the fire towers of Arizona. In standing watch, some lookouts see the trees, some the fire, but this man defines the job as 'freedom'. Freedom to set a schedule and to make decisions without a boss looking over his shoulder.

It would be a long way for the boss to come and check on exactly what the lookout at Monte Vista is contemplating. There are no roads to the summit. Instead three trails make their way up the steep slopes of Monte Vista Peak to this modern live-in tower. The lookout must carry his gear and supplies over a four and a half mile trail. His water is hauled by foot from a nearby spring. A pack mule might re-supply a few groceries along with the propane to fire up a small stove but it is a spartan lifestyle. Due to the long commute by foot he works ten days and then takes four days off. When the season closed in Arizona, he planned to head for the mountains of Idaho to finish the year as a lookout in another remote location.

The area is popular with hikers. We met several people along the trail, hiking past the tower to other points in the Chiricahuas. It is up to the lookout whether he will allow visitors into the visitors. He won't say whether he misses people at his isolated post.

As we looked down the long slope towards the plains below, we talked about the fires that have swept through the Chiricahuas. He pointed over to a ridge that defined one horizon and described the flames dancing along the ridge line in the last major fire. That year's lookout stayed until the last moment, reporting the development of the fire. When the time came, he called for a helicopter to lift him to safety. They plucked him off the peak as he ran down the trail from the approaching flames. The fire did not sweep over the entire peak as much of the forest still remains untouched.

On most districts, it is the lookout who often makes the decision as to how long they will stay when threatened by fire. Some choose to leave early, allowing the air crews to monitor a fire's progress while others claim ownership of the forest in the face of a roaring giant, reporting its every move.

Monte Vista

Coronado National Forest

Mount Bigelow / Coronado Nat'l. Forest

Tower: Mt. Bigelow
Year Built: 1958
Height: 53'
Manufacture:
　Army CL100-106

Model: R-6 flat, 14 x 14 cab
Elevation: 8500'
District: Santa Catalina / Coronado
Access: Road & Trail
Rating: Semi-active

Mount Bigelow

Coronado National Forest

Given the right visual angle, one might suspect that Mount Bigelow Fire tower is the control center for a launch pad of missiles set to blast off into space. The tower shares its little peak with four communication towers. It overlooks steep slopes that were once thick with tall ponderosa. Then fire swept over the peaks of the Santa Catalinas, not once but twice. The tower now surveys a forest of burnt matchsticks, standing in ragged somber garb, awaiting slow disintegration.

Green ponderosa pine still stand on the southern side of the peak, along the Mount Lemmon Highway. The hum of traffic is increasing as life returns to the community of Summerhaven as homes and businesses are re-built.

Before the fires, Mount Bigelow was used only when the forest was tinder dry and lightening crackled overhead. The tower had been built in the late 1950's. It surveyed the northern side of the Santa Catalinas while Lemmon Rock stood watch over the southern half. With the increasing number of visitors peering out over the landscape from various viewpoints, the need for a full time watch at Bigelow had declined. In close proximity to the Palisades Ranger Station, it was easy for personnel to run up to the fire tower to stand watch for a few hours after a storm.

When the fires broke out on the southern slopes, Palisades Ranger station, below the peak, became a beehive of activity as fire crews scrambled to fight the flames and attempted to save Summerhaven. At first it seemed as if they might succeed but the wind turned and swept the flames through the community, leveling many of the homes to ashes. At one point, crews feared they would be unable to save Palisades and the fire tower. Today, they still stand though it will be some time before they are the center of activity as they were before the fires.

Grasses and brush have begun to sprout across the slopes, softening the dismal skeletons of burnt pine. In time, Mount Bigelow may once again be called to service.

Red Mountain / Coronado Nat'l. Forest

Red Mountain fire tower sits just east of Nogales, in the Patagonia Mountains. The fire chief for that section of the Coronado National Forest describes the access as the worst road in Cochise County. After grinding over exposed rock ledges and the loose rock of the surface of the one lane road with no guard rails, in four-wheel drive low, I would have to agree.

The tower sits on private land, a patented mining claim owned by the Kerr McGee. The tiny summit is also the site for several communication towers, so close they seem to hover over the fire tower. The multiple towers leave very little room for parking and a helio-pad. The tower overlooks the

Patagonia, Huachuca and Santa Rita Mountain ranges thus eliminating the need for a lookout on Miller Peak and Mt. Wrightson. Both were sites of early lookout stations, each accessed by long mule rides or backpacking trips. The cabins at each site have been removed.

The little town of Patagonia spreads near the base of the peak. Visitors frequently work their way up the road, stopping just below the tower to look out over the region. The lookouts note that frequently the visitors seem unaware that they too are under observation.

Watch is stood by one of the few couples working a tower together in the state. They split up the week so that each has two days to pursue other interests. The two story, live-in tower is one of the most recent to be built in the state. They share the tower with two cats who are allowed to ground level only in the mornings so as not to become prey for local wildlife. A catwalk surounds the second story. (no pun intended.) The lower level is cement block while the upper half is steel and glass. The outhouse is two switchbacks down a short trail, a long way in a lightning storm.

Standing watch at Red Mountain is unusual in that the couple actively watch for smuggling activities in the valleys below. High speed chases are common along the narrow dirt roads north of the international border. They are able to direct Forest Service personnel away from these dangerous activities. The lookout also reports fires in Mexico though fire fighting is a much lower priority in that nation. The smoke from Mexico's fire may spread across the border, lowering visibility for the Red Mountain lookout.

Red Mountain

Tower: Red Mountain
Year Built: 1973
Height: 10'
Manufacture:
    USDA Forest Service
Model: L-4 duel cab
Elevation: 6,373'
District:
    Sierra Vista / Coronado
Access: Road
Rating: Active

Coronado National Forest

Couples Working Together

In talking to a store clerk one day, I revealed that I work with my husband. She asked if I liked the arrangement and before I could answer, another clerk standing twenty feet away screamed, "Oh my g__, I would never work with that jerk again!"

Startled, we turned as she strode forward, denouncing her ex-husband. Apparently they had owned a business together. The relationship had not ended favorably. I've often thought of that woman's reaction when considering the relationship of couples working in the close quarters of a fire tower. Just twenty five or even twelve feet square of living space make for close quarters day in, day out. Yet most couples that I've met on the towers seem to enjoy it.

Edward Abby, one of the most notorious lookouts in Forest Service history, wrote, "Men go mad in this line of work. Women too, go mad in the solitary confinement of a mountain peak, though not so readily as men, being stronger, more stable creatures with a lower center of gravity. Perhaps the severest test of a marriage is to assign a man and wife to a fire lookout; any couple who survive three or four months with no human company but each other are destined for a long, permanent relationship. They deserve it."

He was speaking out of personal experience. Each couple has a unique arrangement for how they divide the time. Some spend each day rubbing elbows while others split the days of the week between them. One couple I met on Red Butte was separated during the week, he in Phoenix while she lived in Flagstaff. Working weekends together on a fire tower was a grand reunion. Another couple seemed content to torture each other. She described his hiding rocks in her back pack for the four-mile ascent up the peak to their tower. She discovered the rocks only after reaching the summit. I didn't learn how she tortured him in return but it may account for the hours of busywork he spent on the peak away from the tower.

Red Mountain, east of Nogales, is the domain of Gutch and Kathy Goodwin. After torturously grinding up the one lane rock track to the tower, we spent two hours learning how the Goodwins make the job and their relationship a success.

During the winter, they live in Parker Canyon, two hours to civilization by dirt road. During the summer they reside in a "summer home" at the summit of Red Mountain, working as seasonal employees for the Forest Service as fire lookouts. Their summer home is a fifteen foot square room built on a cement block tower, one story up, accessible by metal stairs. A balcony surrounds the second story. From thirty inches above the floor to the ceiling are glass windows, with a 360 degree view of the horizon. No curtains, no neighbors.

The outhouse is down a cement path, below the peak. Their appliances run on propane. They have a computer but without a telephone line they cannot access the Internet. Winter or summer, they are used to living with limited resources.

Communication towers share the peak and technicians make their way up to the towers to service the installations. One tower has a boom that swings with the wind and resoundingly wacks the side of the building in a high wind. They judge the strength of the wind by whether the impact knocks the books from a shelf mounted on the wall. Their only communication is by hand held, battery operated radio or the drive down one of the worse roads in Cochise County. The four-mile road is a spine jarring, rock grinding obstacle course along hairpin turns with steep drop-offs to one side of the road. Communication regarding traffic is carefully maintained by the lookout. The road is one lane with few pullouts. There are sections of the road where those coming downhill just don't backup. They have the right of way. The only way to install a telephone line would be under the road surface. Either Cathy or Gutch seem to navigate this road at least once a day. Every two weeks Gutch makes a run into Tucson to collect mail, paperwork and supplies.

With such a challenging access, friends don't casually drop in and yet visitors make their up the road on private land, often using ATVs. They sit below the lookout, sharing private moments. throwing rocks and even urinating over the edge. The Goodwins can only wonder whether their visitors have any clue that just overhead is a fire tower. They are under observation.

So, no neighbors, few visitors. How do they survive twenty-four hours a day, seven days a week in just two hundred fifty six feet of space, surrounded by windows where the sun wakes them at dawn each day? They have found that splitting the days of the week work best for them. Kathy and Gutch each take two days out of seven to pursue their own interests, often away from the tower. Over the three day week-

Couples Working Together

Coronado National Forest

231

end, they split the time so that the tower is constantly manned over a twelve-hour shift. They agree they enjoy their time working together but also look forward to sharing what they have learned with the other during their time off.

Gutch, in his free time, walks the trails of the Coronado, seeking unique photos. He offers them for sale at a gallery in Patagonia. Cathy proudly describes a sequence of photos he sold last year showing a pair of vultures mating, followed by a nest with their eggs and finally the adult birds teaching the young to fly. Cathy describes Gutch as a people-person but then laughs and says, "he doesn't think so!" She adds that in small or large gatherings he seems to be the pied-piper for small children and dogs.

Cathy has a variety of interests. She is recording the history of the families that settled the region below the lookout. She makes small books and has a degree in Culinary Arts. She describes herself as a homebody, content to pursue her interests high above the activity in the valleys below. As we talked I noted that she repeatedly set a timer at fifteen minute intervals. With each bell, she surveyed the horizon searching for the tattletale stream of smoke.

She laughs about her first year as a lookout and the effort to make good. She mimics seizing the binoculars and frantically scanning the horizon for smoke. It is more relaxed in the tower these days but the work remains professional.

While the two have very different approaches to work, they share a common concern for the safety of the public and care of the land they survey through their binoculars. Gutch allows his work to extend across the counters. He might pick up a soft drink and it stays where he last sets it. Cathy, in contrast, likes her work neatly contained. She describes herself as a conservationist, rather than an environmentalist. It is an important observation. She is not opposed to land usage. She does not seek to prevent changes to the land below and that may be part of her study of the history of early settlement in Patagonia and along the San Pedro River Valley.

The couple began working for the Forest Service over five years as seasonal employees doing GPS survey work over the roads of the Coronado NF and as relief for the full-time lookout. The second year they helped build fences over the Canelo Hills. The following year they took over the position on the fire tower at Red Mountain full-time. Their season runs from late April to late July, unless summer rains create a need to stay a week or two longer. They may do additional work in other areas for the Forest Service before calling it a season. Then they return to their home in Parker Canyon, coming out for supplies and special events like the Tucson Folk Festival. It has to be quite an event to drive a round trip of four hours, much of it over dirt roads.

While they remain committed to each other, Kathy is certain that the job will change with time. "Gutch may pursue other interests. I might work full-time and then he would be my relief. I'm just not sure how we will work this."

Working Together Con't.

Coronado National Forest

Webb Peak / Coronado National Forest

Tower: Webb Peak
Year Built: 1933
Height: 45.9'
Manufacture: Aermotor MC-40

Model: 7 x 7 cab
Elevation: 10,029'
District: Safford / Coronado
Access: Road & Trail
Rating: Semi-active

I first visited Webb Peak in the early 1990's and returned again after the fires of 2004. Comparing the site of the tower in each of the two visits gave a vivid illustration in how fire fighters aggressively approach a wild fire.

The first visit, we had a pleasant walk through a green forest to the tower from the trail head on a road across from Old Columbine. On the second visit after the fire, the route was closed as was the road to the tower. We slipped along the trail through the forest, looking at the damage left by the fire. Burned totems creaked as the breeze swept the hillside. Charcoal littered the ground and huge gouges remained from the bulldozers the crews had used to fight the fire.

Previously, a narrow two track road had accessed the tower. Now a broad slash in the earth's surface swept up the hill and around the tower, cut by the bulldozers. In the haste, to cut a fire break around the tower, little regard had been shown for vegetation. It could grow back. A few green pines still stood on the little island carved around the structure. The crews did what they had to do under pressure from the unrelenting flames to save the tower.

The forty-five foot MC-40 stood deserted, stripped of the quiet beauty that had once softened its aging appearance. Looking around at the mosaic burn-pattern along the hillside below the tower, I wondered when it would be put into use again. Maybe the Forest Service would just abandon the tower in favor of other methods.

Before the fire, the tower had stood watch over the central Pinolenos, Ash Creek, Old Columbine and the recreation area around the little lake that attracts so many visitors to the summit. While Heliograph is the primary tower for the region, Webb Peak had offered a line of sight into pockets that were not visibly from the taller tower. With a tight budget after fighting the fire, the lookout on Webb Peak became expendible. For visitors to Old Columbine, the tower has been a historic and educational tool not far off the Swift Trail. It is another relic of the CCC from the 1930's.

Webb Peak

Coronado National Forest

West Peak / Coronado National Forest

Tower: West Peak
Year Built: 1933
Height: 45.9'
Manufacture: Aermotor MC-40
Model: 7 x 7 cab
Elevation: 8,670'
District: Safford / Coronado
Access: Road & Trail
Rating: Active

West Peak

Coronado National Forest

West Peak fire tower stands watch over the north end of the Pinolenos, an area far less popular than the busy State Route on the southern end of the range. As we drove up the last few miles below the peak, we marveled at the empty campgrounds and the absence of other vehicles on the road. For lookout Ron Arnold, it was a bit of change too, as he had spent the previous three years at Heliograph Peak, along the popular Swift Trail.

The West Peak tower was built by the CCC in 1933, one of the most productive years for the federal effort in Arizona. When the tower was first erected, Blue Bird Saddle was the end of the road. From the saddle, pack mules ferried supplies and building materials the final two miles to the crew building the tower. Fire lookouts also followed the route to the tower. In such a remote location, early lookouts took little time away from the tower so their supplies were packed in by mule. One can only imagine, the anticipation as a fire lookout noted the progress of pack mules being led up the trail to the tower with his supplies ran low.

Though the road has been extended to the summit, hikers may still park at Blue Bird Saddle and hike two miles to the tower, a pleasant up hill climb through tall ponderosa. As the last stretch of road is a bit steep, this isn't a bad idea. It allows us to walk a historic route from the 1930's.

The construction crew built a small two room cabin for the lookout on a saddle below the rocky knob supporting the tower. During our visit, a large American flag flew from the staff, creating a brilliant contrast in the last hour of sunlight, against the green forest and rocky peak. A steep path climbed the rocky summit to the tower from the cabin. Running up and down the trail several times a day would improve the physical fitness of a lookout. Though the cabin is an improvement over a live-in tower, the lookout still has propane and water hauled to the site. And as with the early lookouts, he must look forward to a visit in such a quiet location.

Former Towers / Coronado Nat'l. Forest

Clark Peak
Year Built: 1921
Height: 40'
Manufacture: Forest Service
Model: Wood Tower, 7 x 7 cab
Elevation: 9,006'
District: Safford

Fly Peak
Year Built: 1934
Height: 59.3'
Manufacture: Aermotor MC-40
Model: 7 x 7 cab
Elevation: 9,667'
District: Douglas

Vandalism became such a problem with this tower that it was removed by the Forest Service. Archeologists have recorded the sites of two different towers on the peak based on cement footings. A trail from Rustler Park passes Barfoot cabin then moves on past the site of the Fly Peak tower to the Monte Vista Lookout at the summit of the Chiricahuas. While a road may pass within a half mile of the Barfoot Lookout, all three are accessible only by foot and horseback, a throwback to the early days of the Forest Service.

Merrill Peak
Year Built: 1920
Height: 40'
Manufacture: possibly Aermotor
Model: 7 x 7 cab
Elevation: 9,288'
District: Safford

Miller Peak
Year Built: 1926
Height: 3'
Manufacture: Forest Service
Model: L-4 or L-5 cabin
Elevation: 9,466'
District: Sierra Vista

After repeated acts of vandalism, the decision was made to dismantle Miller Peak lookout, leaving the oversite of the Huachacas between Red Mountain and the Monte Vista lookouts.

Former Towers

Mount Wrightson
Year Built: 1921
Height: 4'
Manufacture: Forest Service
Model: D-6 cupola
Elevation: 9453'
District: Sierra Vista

Mt. Wrightson was the first fire tower built on the Coronado just four years after the Forest Service was founded in 1905. The original structure was a 10 x 10' platform exposed to the elements. A cabin replaced the platform. It was difficult to keep manned due to the long, steep hike to the cabin and the isolation of the watch. It was removed a number of years ago to eliminate it as a target of vandalism.

Mount Lemmon
Year Built: 1913
Height: 30'
Manufacture: Forest Service
Model: CN Wood Tower
Elevation: 9,140'
District: Santa Catalina

Sentinel Peak
Year Built: 1932
Height: 20'
Manufacture: Aermotor MC-24
Model: D-1 cab
Elevation: 9,000'
District: Douglas

Silver Peak
Year Built: 1938
Height: 3'
Manufacture: Forest Service / CCC
Model: L-4 cab
Elevation: 7,975'
District: Douglas

Clark Peak is located north of FR42 as it crosses the Chiricahua Range from the Chiricahua National Monument to the Cave Creek Recreational Area. In 2004 a lightening strike started a fire that destroyed the cabin. The Forest Service learned the tower had been destroyed when the fire was reported by a hiker.

Ladybugs!

The most common visitors for the lookouts have red shells with black spots and a head that retracts into their prothorax like a turtle. Certainly not human visitors. Depending on the wind currents, thousands of lady bugs may be found near our fire towers.

There are more than 5,000 species of ladybugs worldwide with about 450 species in North America. They begin their life cycle when a ladybug lays between fifty and three hundred eggs. The eggs hatch in five days. The ravenous larvae consume aphids, sucking insects that can be so harmful to garden plants. After two to three weeks, the larvae pass through a brief pupa stage before emerging as an adult ladybug, similar to what occurs with a butterfly. At first the ladybug rests, allowing her wings to dry as her spots begin to gradually appear.

As they become active, the ladybugs eat pollen which gives them the strength to fly upward, catching the high atmospheric mid-summer winds that will carry them to the mountaintops. As they approach the mountains, they drop out of the winds into the canyons that course down the steep slopes. The beetles then make their way under their own wing power up the canyons to the summit where they cluster and hibernate on any hard surface. If disturbed from their slumber, the lady bugs may swarm around the intruder, nipping at bare skin. Their bites at most are uncomfortable. They prefer to sleep undisturbed.

Near the end of October, they have used their body fat, gained from the pollen, to hibernate. They awake and start to feed once again on any pollen that remains, dropping into the lower elevations. They must regain the body fat they have lost as it will carry them through a second hibernation. Much to some homeowners discontent, the ladybugs often choose crevices within homes to cluster for this hibernation.

For ladybugs who choose a more natural location, exposure to winter sun in February is important. As the ladybugs wake, they creep under the snow to a location when they can be released from winter's grip. For several weeks they may form a creepy-crawly clump of red bugs until they take wing to seek new locations to lay their eggs, beginning the cycle once again.

The life span of a lady bug is about eighteen months. In our northern climates, they may only be able to complete one egg laying cycle. In the warmer climates, the lady bugs may be able to complete as many as six egg laying cycles in a life span.

Learn more about the ladybug from one of the best sites on the internet by visiting ladybug-fly-away-home.com.

The View From the Outhouse

What follows are some vignettes of events that occurred as we traveled Arizona visiting the fire towers. The accounts do not quite fit with the descriptions of the towers but we have included them with the hope that you find them thought provoking or maybe just entertaining.

But the view from the outhouse!

It had been a tough drive up Red Mountain, low four wheel, the transmission moaning over each rock ledge. Much of the road was one lane with large rocks protruding from the road surface that could rip open the undercarriage of a vehicle. The lookout runs traffic control from above, advising visitors of other vehicles on the road. Most of their visitors are with the Forest Service or the communications companies that share the peak. Their home is a fifteen foot square cabin, one story above ground level, 360 degree windows. The location has its drawbacks as they depend upon propane to power their refrigerator, stove and heater. They depend upon cell phones and radio to stay in touch with the outside world. It is an isolated location!

Gotta go to the bathroom? That's two switchbacks down the hill, following a narrow path to an outhouse. It is a nice outhouse but it still doesn't flush. Yet, the lookout says one of the perks of the job is the view. Sitting on the commode, she can swing the door open to look out across the blue peaks and yellow desert plains topped by a brilliant sky. It may be one of the best views ever from a not so common commode.

Something More to Consider in the Outhouse!

There is only one route to the top of Hyde Mountain. It is a narrow path that climbs a two and a half mile course up the peak. There is little shade and the upper part of the trail is lined with thick brush that may conceal a rattlesnake. We know that because we met one that refused to give up his position on the trail. The small cabin at the summit is rarely used but it remains an official lookout for that extraordinarily dry summer where another set of eyes could be useful in battling a tough fire season.

As a summer storm moved in, we could see the lightning strikes on the plain below and realized that we needed to move to the lower elevations where we would be less exposed than on the open peak. I made a quick trip to the outhouse before we began our descent. Holding my breath, I shut the door behind me and sat down. Looking up at the door, I examined the message scrawled across the surface as I listened to the thunder crack outside the metal outhouse.

> "Shit at your own risk!
> Outhouse not grounded!"

How to Get Even with a Chipmunk

Not all the lookouts are enamored with the small creatures that run across the forest floor. One lookout, who shall remain unidentified, explained that he viewed chipmunks as the vermin of the forest. His cabin stood at ground level and the chipmunks could saunter in the open door and stay a while. He warned me not to move too fast if one made an appearance as it would scamper under the refrigerator. At night, with the lights out, the stowaways make their appearance, dancing across the counters, investigating every cranny, leaving a trail of destruction behind them. It is enough to aggravate the most seasoned lookout.

The master of the forest vermin explained how he evens the score. Sauntering across his cabin, he pulled down a bottle of rum, sloshing a bit into a mug. Then he pulled off a corner of a dried up sandwich and dipped it liberally in the rum before tossing it out onto the rocks below his cabin. Slurping a bit of rum, he tossed another rum soaked crust out to the unsuspecting chipmunks. After two, maybe three, pieces, the chipmunk has begun to lean to one side, sitting very still. And the moment comes when another chipmunk will approach him. It seems that chipmunks are not gregarious animals. There are no social circles by moonlight for the chipmunks. They spend their days chasing each other, stealing from caches and rolling across the landscape in combat. The second chipmunk will take a whiff of the strange odor surrounding the tipsy chipmunk and scurry away. The tipsy chipmunk staggers across the rocks, unable to defend himself or become the aggressor in the chipmunk community until he has a long nap. That is how one aggravated lookout gets even with a chipmunk.

How Not to Meet the Forest Service Fire Teams

It was a quiet trip for the couple who planned a camping trip to the Mogollon Rim near the Baker Butte Tower. They planned a hike and strolled into the forest, leaving their campfire unattended. This was not a wise move. The Forest Service will ticket campers for an unattended campfire. Oh, that they should have been so lucky!

While they were gone, the fire crept out of the circle of rocks, spreading through the grass to nearby shrubs, to their tents and camping gear. Even their vehicles were consumed by the fire. It got the attention of the local lookout and the fire crews. And the couple got the bill for the fire suppression!

And then there were the two old men who went out into the woods to cut firewood for their homes. They pursued a leisurely route, stopping to chat and look over the trees. One even took the time to smoke his pipe, dumping the remains in an old stump. The remains smoldered, eventually igniting the rotted material in the stump and flames began their run through the forest. It is policy to present the guilty party with a bill for fire suppression. It is my understanding, as the story was told to me, that the government took $1.00 from each social security check the man received until the time of his death. Is it true? The story simply makes the point that we must be careful with fire.

The Highway Patrol Works Dirt Roads?

As we approached Diamond Point Fire Tower, we found the gate across the road locked, with a Department of Public Safety officer standing guard as he waited for a swat team to arrive. He informed us that we would not be able to walk up the road to the tower. I asked why this was so as I was reluctant to make another trip to this tower. He informed us that there was a situation involving three men running around the peak with rifles. Eventually we negotiated an

Photo: Mark Caswell

agreement to walk the road in the company of the DPS officer, once the swat team arrived.

As we talked to the officer, the swat team came up the road behind us and I recognized one of the officers when he tapped me lightly on the shoulder. I was astonished to run into him in an official capacity on a peak far from his district. He simply smiled, and with his companions, faded into the forest of pinon and juniper.

After a few minutes, we made our way up the road and my cousin who had accompanied me, heard a voice on our escort's radio ordering the officers to "shoot to kill on first sight." My cousin squealed at me, "Did you hear that?" This was not the suburban life of his first fifty years in southern California.

On a previous trip, we had acquired a flat tire with a hole through a side wall that had sent us back to civilization without visiting all the towers we had scheduled for that trip. Now my cousin asked me if a black cloud followed me on all the trips I planned. I laughed but wondered if there wasn't a bit of truth to his concern. Our escort seemed less than concerned. He seemed to be hiding a smile as he turned off to one side. I wondered if this was for real and I turned back to ask him how this all came to happen. He told me that it was a situation the sheriff's office created. Did that mean the deputies upset these guys running around the woods with rifles or was it all a training exercise?

When we reached the tower, we quickly climbed to the cab as I wondered whether this was a good idea considering there were men with rifles in the woods below us. In talking with the lookout, we learned that she had known about the event for two weeks. We felt a bit foolish to learn that it was nothing more than a training exercise. My cousin nodded, "I thought we got in here a bit too easy." We sauntered back along the road laughing about how I've walked us into one more adventure that his wife was going to find a bit hard to swallow.

What a Tourist Will Do

Among those familiar with the lookouts of Arizona, Shirley Payne at Baker Butte is renown for sewing quilts. She has a modern treadle sewing machine sitting in the cab of her tower forty feet above the ground. Amused, I asked how she got the thing up three flight of stairs. She laughed and admitted, "You would be surprised what you can get tourists to do for you! I gave them all frisbees. I didn't have anything baked that day."

I had the opportunity to sample some of her raspberry pound cake made famous in Joe Bell's book on the lookouts of eastern Arizona. Delicious! Shirley picked the raspberries on her way to work in a special patch near the peak.

As we descended the tower, the ladybugs fluttered around us. She asked what I thought of the lady bugs. I shrugged as the little beetles continued to batter my bare arms. Then I asked what she thought of them after all these years. She replied that at first she thought they were cute, then she resented their stinging bites. Now she just squishes them. (Gandhi be dammed!)

Paper Delivery

Jim Horne is a genial extrovert. He loves getting calls on his cell phone at the Mingus Mountain fire tower to break the monotony in the small seven foot square cab. One of his favorite stories involves the salesman who called from the Arizona Republic and assured him they could have the paper delivered to his doorstep every morning?

"Every morning, my doorstep?" asked Jim, lifting an eyebrow.

"You bet," said the salesman. "We do our best."

"Well, you better get out your pencil for the directions," said Jim. "First, you take I-17 north to the Cottonwood exit."

"Ok, got it."

"Follow SR 260 into Cottonwood and turn north on SR 89, up through Jerome to the summit of Mingus Mountain.

"OK, got it." The salesman was hanging tough.

"Turn left onto Forest Road 104. Now drive just past the church camp and turn right."

For a moment dead silence filled the other end of the line.

"Where did you say you lived?"

Jim laughed at the memory. The man had no idea what finding a fire tower involved. Jim does not get his paper delivered to his doorstep every morning.

A Close Neighbor

There is no easy way to reach the Monte Vista Fire Tower by foot. Three trails climb steep switchbacks to the summit of the peak. Despite the long commute to the tower, we met several people along the trail, hiking past the tower to other points in the Chiricahuas. One older woman, carrying a large pack and accompanied by her dog, left the other hikers in awe over the amount of ground she covered in a short time. Her dog and I had a joyous meeting and he repeatedly ran back to encourage our progress till she had passed beyond the point of easy commuting between the two of us.

We reached the tower only to learn that she had already set up her tent and was on a neighboring peak. The woman, judging by the lines on her face, was older than I and yet her stamina was incredible. We visited the lookout.

We admired the pack animals that stood nearby and envied the contractor the easy ascent. Then we turned to go.

As we descended the long trail, our knees registering protest against the steep descent. We chose to run a few paces along each switchback. As I reached the bottom of a small drainage, I heard a large body crashing through the brush. Stopping abruptly, I peered through the trees at a young bear who was peering through the brush at me. We ducked and weaved, each trying to see the other a bit better. In disgust, he finally turned and began to climb away from me up the slope. I fumbled for my camera tucked safely into my fanny pack but it was too late. He was gone. I was thrilled to catch a glimpse of a bear!

Even the Burros

We drove along State Route 288, north of the little settlement of Young. It is a small community in what was once called Pleasant Valley, the site of a feud between competing parties over grazing rights. The Tewksburys, employed by the Daggs Brothers, had brought sheep into the lush grass of Pleasant Valley over the objections of the cattlemen, led by the Graham Brothers. It turned violent and over 20 men were eventually killed. That was all history until we met five pack mules and their drover strolling along the dirt road known as a state highway. The route follows a historic trail that is still used by migrating herds of sheep each fall and spring as they move between the warm lowlands and the cooler high lands of northern Arizona.

As we visited the Colcord and Aztec Fire Towers we hardly expected to step back into history but the five mules claimed the center of the road. Their

Photo: Mark Caswell

drover slogged along behind them on his own mount with the sheep dogs, tongues dripping in the dust. My cousin, a native of southern California, could hardly believe his eyes. We stopped the car and he took pictures while I spoke to the Mexican drover in Spanish. Just like the history of the sheep drives, the mules moved on.

Calling It a Night

Mack Thomson denies that he gets lonely on Black Rock in the Arizona Strip. He sums it up by saying, "When you go to bed at night, having lost an argument with yourself, you know who to blame!"

He looks up at the myriad of stars in a canopy over his head and feels a sense of contentment creep into his soul. There are no black nights on Black Rock, Arizona.

Index

Apache Maid	74	Jacob's Lake	66	Signal Hill	28
Atascosa	216	Juniper Ridge	134	Signal Peak	198
Aztec	186			Springer Mtn.	143
		Kanabownitz	24	Spruce Mountain	210
Baker Butte	76	Kendrick	52	Sugar Loaf	30
Barfoot	218				
Bear Mountain	120	Lake Mountain	136	Thornton	44
Big Lake	122	Lee Butte	90	Towers	212
Big Springs	62	Lemon Rock	222	Turkey Butte	98
Bill Williams	48	Limestone	162		
Black Pinnacle	104			Volunteer	60
Black Rock	39	Manzanita	46		
Blue	124	Maverick	166	Webb Peak	234
Buck Mountain	78	McFadden	194	West Peak	236
Buckskin	158	McKay Peak	168	Whitney Pass	41
		Mingus	206	Woody Mtn	100
Chediski	160	Mormon Lake	92		
Colcord	188	Monte Vista	224		
		Moqui	94		
Deer Springs	126	Mount Bigelow	226		
Diamond Point	190	Mount Ord	196		
Dry Lake	174	Mount Union	208		
Dry Park	64				
		North Rim	26		
East Pocket	86				
Eldon	82	Oak Ridge	108		
Escudilla	128	Odart	170		
		O'Haco	138		
Fluted Rock	106	O'Leary	96		
Gentry	130	Piney Hill	110		
Grandview	50	Promontory	140		
Greens Peak	132	PS Knoll	142		
Happy Valley	20	Red Butte	54		
Heliograph	220	Red Hill	56		
Hill Top	176	Red Mountain	228		
Hopi	22	Reno	144		
Horse Thief	202	Roof Butte	112		
Humboldt	192	Rose Peak	146		
Hutch Mountain	88	Round Mountain	58		
Hyde Mountain	204				